A
STRAIGHTFORWARD
GUIDE TO

CREATIVE WRITING

STEPHEN WADE

Straightforward Publishing
www.straightforwardco.co.uk

Straightforward Publishing

978-1-84716-608-1

Printed by 4edge www.4edge.co.uk

Cover design by Bookworks Islington

Contents

****

INTRODUCTION

This book is intended to introduce the beginner to the basic skills involved in setting out on the road to success as a creative writer. Creative writing is a term that can mean different things to different people, but I use it here to refer to the writing of fictional or factual works in a variety of forms. If you want to know not only how to write stories or articles but also how to adopt professional practice as a writer, then this book is for you.

I am aware that some readers will be writing already, perhaps even taking a course at a local college or adult education center. This guide may be used to complement such courses; and even if you are the 'kitchen table writer' trying to write with peace and continuity after a day's work, then this will offer you staged workshops involving examples of writing in a range of formats and genres as well as suggestions for further preparatory work.

The openings for prose and poetry have perhaps never been as wide and diverse as they are today. Unfortunately, writing is also attracting more people as a hobby and a potential way of earning money. It is an easy matter to attend short courses and talk about writing, watch television documentaries about writers, read interviews and so on, but this attractive, sometimes glamorous world which the media creates is largely an illusion. The fact is that real writers spend a great deal of time writing - not being media people.

It may take you several years to find out exactly what kind of writer you are, and whether you are able to sustain interest, be able to re-write and so on. The topics covered here will show you exactly what demands are asked of you if you really want to make it as a writer. The word writer does not necessarily mean novelist. By writer I mean someone who can produce publishable quality writing in any given genre or format for a specified readership. Whatever your own aspirations are, though, this guide will offer the basic skills, techniques and knowledge that are essential to success. It is particularly important that you take time over the questionnaire that follows, however, because the more time you spend considering what you want to write and what you are able to write, the less time will be wasted producing the wrong texts for the wrong reasons.

The point to stress here is that imaginative writing depends, in the last resort, on a personal access to your inner resources, and these are a complex mixture of life experience, personal viewpoints and inexplicable visions of life as it could or may be. All this is rooted in the strength of sharing your efforts to understand the multi-layered perplexing creature, Homo sapiens. My personal belief, after several years of planning and teaching courses in creative writing, is that people will succeed if the talent is there, and the talent can only have a chance of being there if encouraged and nurtured. There may be innate qualities of course, as exemplified in Mozart's astonishing creativity at the age of seven. But for most of us, the effort and motivation make our best potential chances of success, and that success has to be defined in your own terms. It may be that you want to write only for your personal satisfaction, and that your work being read by others is not a primary concern.

Questionnaire

What kind of writer have you the potential to become? It is important to ask that question first, rather than the usual one of what do I want to write? General decisions such as will you write fact or fiction are helpful, but this will not resolve the issue as to exactly what you are going to write that will be published. You may not, of course, want to see your work in print, but very few writers settle for the personal satisfaction of simply writing and putting your scripts away in a drawer for 'posterity'. Writing is about communication. You have something to say and you need a way to say it - a form and a set of conventions.

This questionnaire is a set of questions fundamentally about you and your resources, your life-experience and your frame of mind as a potential writer. Just write a few sentences for each question, then decide whether you are suited to write fact or fiction/ journalism or short stories/ radio writing or poems and so on. It is based on the assumption that plenty of thinking time allotted to reflection and soul-searching will reap rewards in creativity. So many people have taken years to discover what categories of writing are best suited to their talents. The sooner you learn your strengths, the better for your sense of purpose. In these questions, then, spend time on the answers, and provide fairly substantial statements. It may even pay to develop these answers into your notebook.

1. What subjects or areas of life most interest you?
2. Are there any subjects you know in reasonable depth?
3. What did your partner/neighbor wear this morning? In other words,
   how observant are you?
4. Fundamentally, do you like people? (take an interest in other lives etc)
5. What magazines and newspapers do you buy regularly and why?
6. What stories in popular culture interest you most? (e.g. films, T.V., popular novels etc)
7. Could you reproduce vocabulary used by teenagers?
8. Do you tend to discuss the plots and characters of novels read/films seen?
9. Are you drawn to biographies or historical works rather than novels? (For the plane or train journey, for instance)

10. Do you spend most time mentally in your past or contemplating the future?

These questions are to ascertain what areas of life or knowledge you could actually write about now; whether you are naturally and instinctively a storyteller or a conveyor of facts. Dr. Johnson said that men more often need to be reminded than instructed - and if your tendencies go along with this, you are perhaps a journalist. If you are sensitive to stories on mass media, perhaps you could write scripts? The point is, what sort of creativity do your answers suggest is within you?

Some Basic Considerations

No matter what you are eventually to write, you also need to ask at this point what attitude you have to creativity and whether you are open to the possibility of knowing yourself. If you are honest about your tastes and abilities, it will not take so long to find the writing type that suits your ability.

Consider these aspects of the creative temperament and ask yourself if you do any of these things as a matter of habit:

1. Keeping a notebook for random ideas and images.
2. Being aware of publications, current trends in fiction or journalism etc.
3. Search out talks by writers, attend short courses in writing.
4. Read and discuss the stories, which capture the popular imagination.
5. Take an interest in your own past experience as possible 'material'
6. Monitor and record the reasons why you admire your favorite writers.

Today, the situation is full of possibilities, at least in the first stage of writing, at which the learning frame of mind is keen and receptive to new ideas. The internet provides a dizzying range of sites devoted to writing, and it is not difficult to join in such things as critique groups, in which other writers give feedback on your work and you do the same for them. It is also easy to find outlets for writing in online magazines, and these are ideal places to begin the essential skills and good habits involved in building up communications lines with editors, publishers and other writers. Every stage of writing is one at which new learning takes place, if one is open to consider new ideas and influences: some may be absorbed and some will be dismissed, but it is the openness that counts.

****

Chapter 1

You as a Writer

Your range and material

Creative writing is a term that covers so many different forms and conventions that one of the first things you need to do is decide exactly what you want to write. Having done the introductory questionnaire, you should have given some time to weighing and considering your strengths as a potential writer. Start now with this process of defining your writing profile. Do you want to write?

- ❖ Fact or fiction?
- ❖ Full length works or shorter forms?
- ❖ According to set types of writing or your own way?
- ❖ Primarily for payment or for your own satisfaction?
- ❖ Working on your own, or by attendance at courses etc.?

All these questions need some careful study. This book assumes that you want to get into print in order to achieve these things: a) payment and b) the satisfaction of seeing your name in print.

What you need to succeed

Most of all, you need determination and ability. But in addition, you have to have a good market sense of what people read and why; you need to understand editors and publication factors, and you need a competence with using language in a clear and effective way. The basic question is how do you know you have the ability? Many people assume that writing is easy as long as you have 'inspiration' but no one is quite sure what this is.

The fact is that you need to know exactly what skills are needed for the kind of writing you wish to do.

An example:
You might want to write short stories. Here is a checklist of a sensible way to establish whether or not you have the potential to be successful:
1. Go to classes and do a short course in fiction writing, or use a guidebook.
2. Read widely and assess what ingredients make a readable story
3. Write a draft of a story and get feedback (from tutors, students or even professionals - who charge you, of course)
4. Submit your story to six editors. If they all reject you, ask some basic questions again about your methods.

Ways of Working

There are as many ways of going about writing as there are writers, but there is some common ground. These are the rules:

❖ Establish research methods of your own (see chapter 2).
❖ Monitor editors' responses.
❖ Do market research and up-date yourself on outlets.
❖ Write to a disciplined timetable.
❖ Understand the language and style adopted in your chosen writing category.

All writers have to have a strict timetable and keep to it. Work at the time of day that most suits your energy and other commitments. Never try to work for very long periods without regular breaks. Do contrasting activities in order to unwind. Keeping a log of what you write and for whom is sensible advice.

Some preliminary questions

These are the most common questions asked by aspiring writers, regardless of whether they wish to write novels, articles, scripts and so on:

1. Is it possible to guarantee publication?

Answer: No, but you can do your best to increase your chances. You can present accurate and neat typescripts, send material to the right outlet and write according to guidelines of style.

2. What are my chances of earning a living by writing?

Answer: Not very great. But writing is definitely a useful source of supplementary earning; it is not too difficult to write with some reasonable financial success if you go about it methodically and with a clear purpose.

3. Can an amateur understand the publishing world?

Answer: Of course, there seems to be a huge amount of information at first, which is rather jargonised and sounds very official. Words such as copyright and royalties, proof reading etc. But the fact is that your main concern is to write well. If an editor wants your material, help will be given to you. Ask questions and establish a working relationship with those who express an interest in what you write.

4. What if I fail?

Answer: If you ultimately fail, even after working with forethought and attention to detail, then at least you have tried to do what some instinct in you has urged you to try. This applies with all the arts. But there are so many varieties of writing, that some small modicum of success is open to virtually all who try and persist. Remember that failure in writing only relates to what you set out to do. If you demand no less than to win the Booker Prize, then disappointment and failure are likely. But if you want to write ten articles a year for magazines, your chances of success are quite high.

Your notebook.

There has been a massive growth of interest in the art of journaling, particularly after the impact of Tristine Rainer's book, *The New Diary* (1978). Although this course was based on journaling as a reflective diary of self-development, it is essentially very similar to the writer's notebook. Why should you keep a notebook? Mainly because it is a way of logging spontaneous reactions and observations from the constant flux of life flowing by you.

Be a Flaneur

Your notebook may be an amalgam of notes, plot ideas, observations, press cuttings and even passages of writing that may have been written in the most unusual and unscholarly places. For instance, I started one of my best stories sitting in a café in Yorkshire; a sequence of poems was started by a lakeside in Canada, and I have a notebook of 'false starts' which were written in cafes and parks from Cumbria to London.

The pace of modern life is such that we rarely meet eye to eye and the most common experience of others is a blur as they speed past us in a city center. For a writer, this is anathema. There is a lot to recommend the habit of sauntering. In the mid-nineteenth century, the French poet, Gerard de Nerval practised the art of the flaneur: this is to walk slowly, taking in the sensations of the world, seeing the potential for art in every piece of data and experience. He kept a lobster on a lead, thus forcing an extremely slow rate of movement. If post-modernity is partly about the estrangement from the world through technology, then perhaps it is necessary for the writer to stand against that wave and be a Canute of the imagination. So much art springs from human contact rather than abstract ideas, and taking time to observe closely provides some of the best research for writing: often far more profitable than work in a library.

The Importance of Being Contemporary

You might think that great literature is written by people with a deep knowledge of the classics. This is a common assumption in writing classes. But have you ever considered just how much successful novelists, journalists or poets owe to their sense of the contemporary and to their immersion in popular culture? Think about that wellspring of material that percolates from this familiarity with the modern idiom. First, this knowledge ensures that your vocabulary will be credible; it also allows for definite and easy research as it is based on people, and they are all around you.

An interesting case study in this respect is Raymond Chandler. Arguably, one of the most useful books any aspiring writer might consult is The Notebooks of Raymond Chandler (see bibliography for full details). Here, we have a record of Chandler's progress and a file of his research methods. Remember that Chandler was educated in the classics, at Dulwich College, England, and that it was only when he discovered the hard-boiled crime fiction of *Black Mask* magazine in the kiosks that he realized what category of storytelling was made for his talents. His notebooks contain lists of similes, drug and police slang, physical descriptions, openings, story lines and titles. It provides a rare insight into the mental workings of a writer who knew his readership, and who had managed to find the fulfillment of his creative vision in an established popular format.

We are not all that lucky; but was it luck? Reading these notebooks, it becomes obvious that the real secret of his success was hard work and dedication, but he had to know somehow what was his metier from the start. How do you find out what your most suitable writing category is, without wasting time trying what you are poor at? You might:

* Trust your instinct, and use your reading life as an exemplar.
* Obtain professional feedback on some of your writing.
* Join a creative writing class specifically in your current writing and accept comments.

But in the end, what every writer aspires to is a melding of instinctual vision and professional practice. Chandler made his own success in that respect, without the need of a degree in literature or evening classes.

Now read the KEY POINTS from Chapter One

****

KEY POINTS FROM CHAPTER ONE

YOU AS A WRITER

- Think carefully about what you want to write and why. Write a checklist of your interests and what you would enjoy writing. Think of what you, as a reader would like to read.

- Test the ground first by reading widely and find out about courses to supplement this book.

- Set achievable targets and be realistic.

- Plan methods of working and a timetable that suits you. Be disciplined in your approach.

Now turn to chapter two

Chapter 2

Basic Skills

Having thought about the organization and planning involved in launching your writing career; you are now ready to take stock of your ability to use language accurately and to a set purpose.

Language knowledge

Regardless of what you want to write, there are certain pre-requisites for effective and directed writing. You need to be aware of the guidelines for clear and accurate usage in language, issues of vocabulary and how your selected language and style relate to the imagined reader. These topics are summarized here briefly.

Grammar and usage

If you have never thought about these before, now is the time to do so. Grammar refers to a set of widely accepted rules of how words are used and how sentences and other word-groups are linked and inter-related. In traditional terms, grammar was prescribed. That meant that there were fixed rules we should all follow. Now there is more conviction behind the idea of a descriptive grammar - a system that describes what usage's are contemporary and seen as being good communication. The clear and efficient communication of your ideas and feelings is the point. Usage is the word used to describe the way we use language by instinct and convention, without following the rules. What you need to know as a writer is the basic material for accuracy. You need to know:

How to use words in the right place and order so that there is no ambiguity - no double meaning.

How to write clear sentences, not too long and involved, nor always too short.

How to refer to time - use verb tenses well.

This is a minimum checklist of guidelines. To build on this, you should invest in a handbook of basic grammar such as *Good Grammar in One Hour* (Sunday Times/Mandarin 1993) or any similar publication.

Guideline one

Keep to one main idea in each sentence. That is, have one subject that is referred to.

Guideline two

Never write long, complex sentences. As a rule of thumb, never go beyond three related pieces of information about your main subject.

Guideline three

Keep to the same verb tense. If you are talking about an event in a particular time, use the same tenses - past or present or future tenses. Only use a mix of tenses when there are aesthetic reasons, of course, to do with narration or the treatment of the subject.

Guideline four

Use plenty of pronouns. If you are writing about John, don't keep saying 'John'. Use his, him, he etc. These are pronouns, standing in place of the word 'John'.

Guideline Five

Use adjectives and adverbs correctly:

An adjective describes a noun: The red house.

An adverb describes a verb: He ran quickly.

So never write:' The car moved quick' and so on unless it is in dialogue.

Vocabulary

There are very helpful tips to be found in this area. Choose words that are suitable for the readership, the setting, the character or the age group. Good vocabulary is all about selecting and rejecting from the massive stock of words at your disposal. The most useful practice in this context is to use a thesaurus as well as a dictionary. One simple exercise will illustrate:

Suppose you want to use an adjective to describe an old, interesting building in a piece of factual journalism. Your sentence might be as follows:

'The old mill had only a few remnants visible of what it was like in its pristine state in 1740'.

What you want to do is be more concise. Do you add another 'long word' and change it to:

'The old mill had only vestiges of its pristine state as it was in 1740'.

In other words, you need to consider some basic contrasts in vocabulary and use your discretion to select the ones that best suit your purpose. Often this process of selection is natural and easy, but the search for the right word often needs more than a thesaurus. These contrasts are:

1. Latinate......................English
2. abstract......................concrete
3. Specific......................general

Examples might be operative/worker= latinate/English.   Honesty/

ideology/freedom = abstract words.   Table, pen, grass = concrete words.

The crumbling, dilapidated wall = specific / The broad walls of the town=general

Of course, this is an over-simplification. There is no formula that will guarantee the best way to write your specific text. All you can do is study the best models for your genre of fiction of category of factual writing. All the standard guidelines containing supposedly 'golden rules' about language and style are broken by writers of genius, of course. Many outstanding writers have succeeded by using words, which have traditionally been outside the accepted language of literature. James Kelman, for instance, won the Booker Prize partly on the strength of his originality in boldly using the Glasgow vernacular as it exists and by eschewing 'literary' style and embellishment.

These are just a few of the most important issues of language to be aware of. But the best way to learn is to read widely and to keep a check on what words are constantly being generated in your area of interest as a writer. If you write articles on, say, football, you need your own vocabulary list. This might include slang, terrace songs, insults, new trendy sportswear and so on. You have to make this wordlist your top priority if you want your writing to be convincing and up-to-date.

Research sources

A writer needs to be aware of all potential sources of information for use when the preparation stage for writing has to be organized. You need a workable knowledge of these sources:

❖ Library materials: book and non-book
❖ local or professional contacts
❖ Specialist services such as photo-libraries

❖ facts relating to your specialist area
❖ computer based data.

The best advice is to compile your own materials in various forms. Many journalists, fiction-writers and factual writers keep indexes and cuttings etc. The first step is to acquaint yourself with exactly what services are available to you.

Knowing your market

Whatever you write, you need to know what markets are available, what might open up in the near future, and which aspects of the perceived market are shrinking/expanding. Keep a check on the library and bookshop shelves. Most of all, be aware of the range of options. For instance, if you write on popular music, any shelf of a good newsagent's shop will show you the range of styles, all aiming at certain musical tastes in specified readership-groups. You will need to read all these first, and monitor the differences in house style. That is, what vocabulary and type of sentence-structure is favored by each magazine; what images match the words and what lifestyles and attitudes are reinforced in the texts. There are also, of course, professional publications to help freelance writers here. *Writing Magazine* is one of the best, available without subscription, this has specialist articles on all types of writing from children's stories to hymn-writing and local history. A magazine such as Bookseller will give you the statements made by professionals in the publishing industry. There is also a growing number of professional journals and magazines attached to writers' organizations, such as the Romance Writers of America, which publishes the *Romance Writers' Report*, full of writing advice and market information.

In the USA the proliferation of short courses and writing programs in all aspects of writing give aspirant writers the chance to meet and learn from published authors, and there is also a great deal of on-line help now. (see the reference section for website addresses)

Keeping records

Most important of all is the need to keep records particular to you and your interests. These are some of the methods used by writers in all areas of work: (all methods are useful, with or without a word processor and the wonders of computer-disk storage.)

- ❖ cuttings from newspapers and magazines on your topics
- ❖ photo-files for characters in fiction
- ❖ notes on fashion, hair, technology etc.
- ❖ market or subject features from professional journals
- ❖ interviews with writers you might learn from or use as 'models'
- ❖ features on new outlets
- ❖ statistics

You will soon learn what sources are open to you for such information. The important thing is to be systematic. You might use an index book for up-dating market outlet addresses; a display book with transparent pockets for photo-cuttings and a loose-file for other press-cuttings. Some fiction-writers pin up photos of character-types, so they are always visible, on a cork-board.

The other type of indispensable record is a log of submissions and editorial feedback you might simply do this:

Item.........................Publication........   Date   sent..........
Accepted/comments

All comments, however brief, from editors, are extremely useful. Some editors are always too busy to give you more than the usual rejection slip. Others will give a one-line reason for rejection, and even something like 'Too detailed' will prove useful.

A Reader's report

You may have so little helpful feedback from busy editors that you are willing to pay a moderate sum for a professional reader's report. These are usually ex-agents or employees of publishers who have set up their own small business. For your money, you receive an in-depth analysis and feedback comments on your writing, with its suitability for being published, and advice on how and why to change, re-write or amend certain elements in the style or subject. These readers advertise in the annual handbooks, on websites and in national writing magazines. Many are in close contact with agents, and have an impressive track record of successful authors.

Now read the KEY POINTS from Chapter Two.

****

KEY POINTS FROM CHAPTER TWO

BASIC SKILLS

- Check on your ability with language and work on any weaknesses. Use a short grammar book.

- Invest in good reference works such as a thesaurus and dictionary and use them to back up practice drafts of writing. Practice with alternative versions.

- Always up-date market information. Be constantly aware of changing trends in publishing and log trends.

- Produce your own record-keeping materials and methods. Always up-date these at every writing session. Be consistent in this.

Now turn to Chapter Three

Chapter 3

Writing Fiction

Now that you have a clear idea of what you want to write and what language skills are required as a definite basis for work, you are ready to consider the fundamentals of writing fiction. This could cover anything from short monologues to full-length novels, so the present chapter covers the writing skills that cover all types and forms.

Point of View

Telling a good story is the basis of all the art and craft involved in writing fiction. When we tell stories verbally, in anecdotes and jokes, there is no need to take special care with planning a form and a structure; we have gestures, movements and humor to add to the telling. But when you shape a story in print, you immediately note the difference. The writer has to give a coherent development to the progression of the story, keeping the tension and interest all the way. How is this done?

There are at least three common methods of telling (*narration*).
1. Use a narrator - first or third person as a rule
2. Tell the story in 'the authorial voice'
3. Start in the middle of the action and dramatize

Narrator and third person

Ist person I /me/my
3rd person he/she

Notice the difference in the effect in this contrast of two ways to start a story:

1. First person
I've been working in a factory for three years now, and I'm sick of it. I'll do anything to find a way out. I'm going nowhere in a nowhere job.
2. Third person
He was restless and unhappy. His factory work was boring him and the restlessness was getting worse.

Notice the difference. The first person takes the reader closer to the person at the center of the story. The third person distances him.

The authorial voice
This gives the writer a chance to say anything at any time. You can refer to what is happening in the character's head or give factual information, geographical details and so on. For instance, this could be the opening of a story:

'The woods in the south of the area were wild. Wolves had been seen and heard in them. Few men ventured there alone. It was the most barren part of a lawless land'.

This method allows you to have the ultimate flexibility in all areas. You can add anything at any time. The only problem is that with choice comes the multiplicity of options. You might need to plan carefully, deciding exactly what to select and what to reject.

In the middle
With this style, the writer stresses the drama at the opening. You begin

in the thick of the action, perhaps with dialogue or with plenty of movement and sound:

'Crack..... the shot rang out across the clearing. John ducked and kept low in the undergrowth. He had the feeling that he was surrounded and that it was the Kennedy gang, out to take more from him than his wallet'.

What they all have in common is that a viewpoint is created. Plan carefully, when you have your characters and plot, deciding what viewpoint is to be stressed. You need to decide what to foreground. How do you want the reader to perceive, sense and respond to the events you depict? Put yourself in the place of the reader.

Using a narrator is a subtle device, of course. You can make the storyteller 'unreliable'. That is, the reader develops an attitude to the teller, as the story builds up. If you give your narrator a personality, you open up great possibilities for irony and subtle characterization. You can enjoy creating a teller of a story who has a 'vested interest' in the events - an attitude to them which creates tensions.

Plot and character

Right at the heart of storytelling is the issue of whether to let your fiction be plot-driven or character-driven. It might be helpful here to talk about 'plot' stories and 'art' stories and to decide which suits you the better.

'plot' story

This relies on plenty of events and a definite climax, often dramatic or a 'twist'.

'art' story

This relies on one event, and puts more stress on character, setting, mood etc. It may be impressionistic.

Plot

This refers to the interplay of events and people. Some writers approach the task by carefully working out the sequences of plots and sub-plots, and how and why characters change and develop as events happen. This assumption here is that if you keep the reader reading, you have succeeded. As Willie Collins put it, 'Make them laugh, make them cry, but most of all, make them wait.'

Everything has to be logical, fully explained and believable, of course, in this. You need to be sure of all facts and re-read carefully before sitting down for each writing-session.

Character

Some writers work on the principle that people create events. That is, if you create a character or characters of sufficient depth and interest, then the events will follow naturally. You imitate the tensions and conflicts of reality. You can work in this way by creating an imaginary c.v. for the main characters. The idea is that, if you know the people you make well enough, you should instinctively 'know' how they would react in a given situation.

The guidelines for this approach are as follows:

Write copious notes on the characters before writing.
Use photos or 'models' from real people where possible.
Research their clothes, education, work, hobbies etc. very thoroughly.

Description

This is a fiction-writing skill which is under-rated and taken for granted, yet few writers are aware of the incredible range of choices open to you as a writer when you need to describe a person, a place or an object. Basically, you need to be aware of these methods.

1. Use visual, sensual vocabulary where possible.

For instance, when describing a place, give more than shape, color and perspective. Add sounds, words that evoke what is special. It might be the smell in the air near a steelworks or a brewery - or even a busy road. Find the particular.

2. Find a simple image. For instance, a road after heavy rain might be described in this way:

'The road glistened as if coated with lacquer.'

3. Give a response rather than a bland account. What reactions does the place/person evoke in another character - or even in a passer-by seeing the place/person in a desultory way?

Basically, read widely in your chosen category and learn from the practitioners.

Monologue and dialogue

A helpful way to start writing fiction is to try a monologue. This is a story in the first person, usually short, with just one voice speaking - no real secondary characters being there. (See Alan Bennett's 'Talking Heads)'.Work in this way:

1. Write brief character notes on a person you have seen or that you have often noticed - a local 'character' perhaps.

2. Note some of the typical things they might say in conversation.

3. Place them in a specific setting that they can refer to.

You don't really need a story line for a monologue - you can simply describe a state of mind. The person might be waiting for a very important caller or telephone call. The tension is there in the waiting, from your first line. The advantage of this is that you can write just one page and see how far you can develop personality in a few hundred words. For example:

'I don't know why I do this... wait for him to ring, I mean. He'll be down the pub playing snooker and throwing pints down his gullet. Tea's been in and out of the oven six times.... and I sit here and take it, week after week... why? It's time I asked myself that question a bit more seriously....'

Note how this need not have any apparent direction, even though it might have been meticulously planned before writing the first word.

Dialogue is a different matter. This is a skill to practice as often as possible. What functions does dialogue serve? The word refers to a conversation, so what can be done, in a story, with such a device? Every fiction has lots of conversation, of course:

It moves the story on;
It gives information about people;
It gives background information;
It adds variety of presentation.

Bad dialogue is that which is not there for any purpose. Why include this, for instance -

'Good morning Sam.'
'Morning Mr. Kelly.'

It does nothing. But this snatch of talk does a lot:

'I was wondering if you might lend me your car, dad...' Joe mumbled.

'What? Speak up lad.... you'll never get anywhere in this life if you're not heard.'

This little interchange adds a great deal to the reader's notions of the relationship, and to individual personalities.

In writing dialogue, the secret is to use sparingly and wisely, when things need to be said subtly or indirectly, or when you want to show a feature of someone. In fact, the saying of Show, don't tell is generally a useful guideline in writing stories.

But where do ideas come from?

These skills and approaches are all very handy, but only if you have ideas. That is the commonest complaint in a creative writing course. How do you find something to write about? Writers divide, perhaps, into two basic categories: the 'natural' storyteller who goes in search of stories all the time, and the 'craftsperson' who works more from the study, theory and other writers than from observed life itself. Which are you? There are strategies you can use to invite stories 'to happen' as it were.

First, always rely on working out a basic tension or conflict. Work on the eternal stories that never change - stories about loss, parting, loving, believing and the extreme emotions.

Second, invent characters whom you 'know' well from observation and experience.

Third, don't re-invent the wheel. There are only so many stories (31, according to one literary theorist). For instance, there are potential stories all around you.

Fourth, if totally stuck, take an idea from a newspaper report of an event and fictionalize it. Nowadays, the word faction has been created to account for the stories on the borderline of fact and fiction, which are so popular. After all, how does an autobiography differ from an autobiographical novel?

Finally, remember the point about a story told - an anecdote - and ask yourself how you can preserve the power and immediacy of that. For instance, consider this story, told in a few sentences - a minisaga(a form invented by the science fiction writer, Brian Aldiss)

The Blind Girl who Loved all things Yellow

'She loved deeply and foolishly. She loved the spring, though she could see no colors. She adored, especially, all yellows. The primroses in spite of their smallness, and the daffodils, even though they were common stuff in poetry. And most of all, she loved him, as he never introduced her to his friends'.

Work on stories that draw your own imagination to them, and begin with stories of your own friends and neighbors. Turn the real very gradually into the unreal. After all, poets are all liars, as Plato said.

A workshop example

The kind of stimulus for short stories that you might find in a course workshop can be reproduced to some extent here. The structure of this might be as follows, and all it requires is a good A4 notebook and a quiet place to work:

Write a passenger list for an imagined voyage (base it on The Mayflower). Invent occupations for each person; make families; then state how they died. Arrange for a mini-story line involving any two of these.

Write a short episode – say 700 words, mixing dialogue and

description.

The useful aspect of this exercise, as a warming-up piece for your fiction writing, is that is uses the randomness that we find in the actual process of storytelling. Your episode could turn out to be almost any genre. (It often becomes a comedy in my classes!)

Now read the KEY POINTS from chapter three

****

KEY POINTS FROM CHAPTER THREE

WRITING FICTION

- Understand and practice different approaches to writing a point of view. Find the one that you enjoy most.

- Decide on whether plot of character-driven stories suit your abilities and habits of thought the best.

- Use a range of descriptive skills, particularly on people and places.

- Write a monologue as a first step, based on a known person.

- Cultivate a method of gathering potential ideas for plots.

Now turn to Chapter Four

Chapter 4

Factual Writing

Writing stories does not match everyone's tastes, and you may be better equipped to succeed in the area of factual writing. This may be in freelance journalism, or in local history. The range is very wide and all the options are expanding at the moment.

Varieties and styles

Writing facts is a very simplified way to express a variety of creative writing which allows you to specialize in topics you know and enjoy. These are some of the options:

- Writing feature articles
- Doing interviews and profiles
- Specialist writing
- Current affairs
- Leisure and hobbies
- Instructional writing

Regardless of your dreams of being a writer with a national reputation, start by being realistic and ask yourself what the situation of a factual writer is. First, you are in competition with professional journalists and those 'house' writers who write regular features or columns with specific magazines and newspapers. So how do you choose from the above varieties? Do the following.

1. Write a checklist of the areas of life that you know well. That is, what subjects could you talk about now, 'off the top of your head'?

2. Write down a list of information sources of which you are aware. How easy would it be to access information on your chosen area/areas of interest?

3. Do some market research both locally and nationally, as to the existing material in print on the subject.

4. Draft out a short article and ask for the response of the local editor of your town newspaper.

Some examples

This might be a case study. Suppose you know a lot about photography, simply as an amateur. The existing glossy magazines that you may find on the shelves of your local newsagent do take freelance contributions, but you are up against some stiff competition. Then move down to the general interest publications that have some items on photography. Assess their typical subjects, then try one for that outlet first. Finally, start local. Offer to write a column for your local paper on 'Photography for Starters' for instance.

In other words, most factual subjects tend to come under these categories:

(a) Specialist
(b) General but national
(c) Local
(d) Amateur.

The amateur publications will be a start, but not really much of an advance. This might be the case with, say, the photocopied magazine of

38

a local group of enthusiasts. I know of several writers who started by writing a chatty but informative column in their local newspaper.

Style
You need three basic abilities to write well on subjects with a factual basis:

Good research skills.
A balance of entertainment and fact.
An 'angle' which is reader-friendly.

Research skills for your specific subject may involve either confirming knowledge you have already, or finding out about a detailed area of knowledge from texts or experts. You simply need to create good communication systems with reference librarians, keep a cuttings file and have a notebook of your own with the essential body of facts for your subject coherently summarized. You need facts at your elbow as you write. With some subjects, a solid textbook will have everything (a dictionary of geology for instance would be useful to a writer on travel and topography) but most factual subjects change over time - often rapidly. The classic example is law. Supposing you write on legal matters for the self-employed. You need to be updated all the time, and have good sources.

Entertaining with facts is a rare skill. Consider these three openings to an article on collecting samplers:

1. Samplers found in most antique shops will be mostly Victorian and often in very bad condition. Be careful when you buy them.
2. My first sampler was found in a ragbag but now sits proudly on my wall: 'Hannah Smith did this: 1875'.

3. Read all the books first, then consider collecting, but specialize in a period, a style or a size.

The second opening has just a hint of fun, and it conveys a slice of reality by quoting. The other two are predictable. You need a suggestion of personality behind the facts. Give your reader facts in discrete, well-positioned morsels, not all grouped together. A reader needs time to absorb, so dress up the facts in some anecdotes or gives examples from real life. Put no more strain on the reader than you would if you were talking, rather than writing, the words.

As to creating an 'angle' - this is the toughest task you will face. Supposing you have three basic facts to put in your opening paragraph on one of a series of pieces on 'Great Playwrights of Our Time':

Harold Pinter writes about intense relationships - uses a room as a setting - menace in his themes. You might write these three notes into an angle of sarcasm:

Pinter's name will always be associated with dramas in which aggressive people, who feel trapped by their identities and relationships, pace about a bare room like panthers looking for a red steak.

Interviews and profiles

Many freelance writers work from interviews and always write about the one subject that never fails to be interesting - people. In historical studies, Oral History has become a whole area of interest, with interviewers recording conversations with senior citizens on matters of social history, witnessing of events, or simply everyday life in days gone. There tend to be three types of interview/profile open to you:

1.   A character profile - strong human interest

2. Profile of a celebrity - even a local celebrity.
3. A historical or documentary subject.

Whichever you choose, be sure to read model writing first. For instance, the Chicago journalist Studs Terkel has specialized, in his long life, in interviewing people from all walks of life, and his approach has been to let their characters shine through. Why write your own imaginative angles when ordinary talk sparkles with slang, dialect and colorful emphasis?

If you choose a character profile, you need to look for someone who has undergone a testing, hard experience. It might be a fund-raiser for charity (local press outlet) or it might be someone in your town who has taken part in some national event (The London Marathon?) and you might find a real story there.

A celebrity profile means that you interview and write about anyone who has achieved wide recognition - even fleetingly - and is of passing interest. Common potential subjects in this category might be a relative of someone famous, someone who has just entered the *Guineas Book of Records,* or even an artist with a current exhibition somewhere. The point is that these people want a good press, and you are seen as a friend.

The historical interview means that you need to have a proper interest in social /local history. You need to ask relevant and informed questions. Do some preparatory reading before doing the interview. But this type is the easiest to undertake, because absolutely anyone will have a story. Take, for instance, a woman who has been a nurse all her life and who has just retired. Think of the stories in her head, and also her witness to change in a career full of human drama.

Obviously, in all interviewing, there are some basic guidelines:

Prepare well, and research the topic.
Write your questions before hand.
Make all questions open-ended (answered by a full statement, not yes or no.)
Be relaxed and make the interview informal and fun.

If this is your type of writing, you might want to invest in a micro-cassette recorder as well as in the traditional notebook. With this, you can place it unobtrusively in the room, still writing in your notebook and chatting. But you have a record of every word said, so you can edit later, and summarize the factual content in the answers. Remember the other factors in any interviewing process:

Keep eye contact.
Always seem interested.
Be aware of the comfort of the interviewee.
Limit your time and keep to it.

Profiles and features on people always have one simple advantage over general factual writing - people are involved, so you are able to give subjective responses and natural-sounding memoirs.

Documentary and features

A documentary style or format normally means that the writer puts the stress on facts, hard realism and on important issues concerned with how life is or has been experienced. One of the most famous documentary film-makers, John Grierson, defined it as 'the imaginative interpretation of reality'.

Writing in a documentary style means that you put the effort into those aspects of writing which will make the reader feel a sense of confrontation with areas of life which are not normally experienced so easily.

For that reason, a documentary approach has to use these techniques:

a wide variety of descriptive methods;
a sense of drama;
immediacy in dialogue;
startling imagery;
some rhetorical devices such as over-stating.

This paragraph is an example, based on the topic of commuting:

'Kevin is usually awake and alert at six a.m. He has to drive to work and the trip takes an hour and a half. He's tried all the alternative routes, trying to shorten the trip. But it takes an hour. He has to be in the car by seven. When he arrives at work he is already tired, a bit frayed at the edges. Then he has to smile and start the real work. He says that 'time in the car gets you thinking and planning... but you always get a thumping headache.'

Note that this is immediate, made dramatic, and uses his actual words. In documentary, you should try to recreate the experience of life as it is felt. The writing should detail all the aspects of experience that make up the total picture - and with human interest.

You need to like research, and you need to have an instinct for how the apparently ordinary may be transformed into a strong human story if documentary appeals to you.

Many writers go looking for stories of suffering and trauma for that reason.

Features
As this word implies, a feature is a central, important factual piece in a magazine or newspaper. When starting out, it is sensible to write a piece of about 700 words on an aspect of life you know well, then try your local paper. Some potential topics might be:

a local person with a success story;
a controversial issue (new by-pass, neighbors' row etc.);
a subject in leisure and recreation;
educational argument etc.

In a feature, you need photography or drawings to really give the piece a central impact. But the writing needs to be a mixture of facts and opinion, with plenty of direct quotation from people involved. A good way of working is to write a list of possible treatments of the subject and then choose which is most suitable. For instance:

Subject: A local lecturer in further education with excellent exam. results.
Possible treatments:
1. He is a quiet man - dedicated to his profession
emphasis - his personality
2. He is well known. A real character
emphasis - other people's views
3. Highly valued in the school
emphasis - his academic side, part played in social life etc.

Then, when satisfied that you have found the best treatment, work on the opening paragraph and start with a quotation from the subject or from something in print.

Reviews

There is always a market for reviews, and often you can create an interest in an editor who has perhaps not previously put much stress on reviews. Some editors have a firm policy of only ever using reviewers who are well known, but remember that there are several kinds of publications. They could be ranked in this order, in terms of being potentially openings for freelance reviewers:

1. The national publications.
2. Specialists who need specialist writers.
3. Regional publications always looking for talent.
4. Age group based publications such as Melody Maker or Country Life.
5. Small scale outlets.
6. Specialist or academic publications.

Basically, you should first decide on what you want to review - books, films, theatre etc., then narrow the field further. Books are a huge reference-word. You might keep to fiction or biography, or simply books that are related to your hobby or profession. Then write a short review of a recent publication. Keep to about 300 words. Submit this to the editors of six magazines, with a covering letter, offering to review books for them in future.

Writing skills in reviewing all turn on the fundamental reasons for publishing a review in the first place. These are:

Giving information regarding 'life and work';
conveying excitement and interest;
stressing the usefulness of the book;
saying why it should be bought, not borrowed;
writing for those in the know   e.g. the latest Patrick O'Brian or Catherine Cookson.

The important thing is to keep yourself well in the background, be objective, and communicate enthusiasm. Do not stress the really negative factors in a book. Criticize weakness by all means, but look for the good points. A review should be a good read in its own right. A reader should feel, having read a review that he or she knows a few facts about the writer, the ground covered, and some background information. Most of all, they should want to read the book immediately.

Poor technique:
Being sarcastic
Negative backbiting
Showing off your superior knowledge
Picking on small details and leaving out the important elements

Good technique:
Stressing the achievements
Giving reasons for reading or not reading
Showing how the books fits in with existing knowledge
Communicating life and enthusiasm

Now read the KEY POINTS from chapter four.

KEY POINTS FROM CHAPTER FOUR

FACTUAL WRITING

- Be aware of the wide range of approaches open to you.

- Check and summarize your own existing knowledge. Relate this to markets

- Use a reliable method of note taking, recording and drafting out work. Have a workable system.

- Never overburden with facts. Include entertaining elements as well.

- In documentary, always include aspects of current or universal human interest

- Have enthusiasm and commitment. Write with energy and variety on all subjects.

Now turn to Chapter Five

Chapter 5

Writing a Short Story: Workshop

We now focus on particular forms of creative writing which you might wish to take as short introductions to the main types of writing undertaken by amateurs, part-timers and beginners. But don't be surprised if you 'take off' and find that you start to earn as well as simply enjoy the process of writing. The short story is the commonest form exploited by most writers when first setting out.

Planning

Writers who ultimately want to dream of writing that first novel start with trying the short story. The earlier chapter took a broad view; this chapter concentrates on the writing process involved in writing a story from idea to script. What are the usual stages? Usually, it goes something like this:

Plot idea / notes on people / summary of events / first draft/ final draft.
There are several ways to gather ideas for plots, but for this workshop, we concentrate on one: the use of a basic situation of conflict and tension. This is the basis of every successful story.

Stage One

Our story concerns two women. One is a nurse who lives and works in Yorkshire. She is thirty and has two children. The other character is her sister, and she has lived in Australia for ten years. She is the elder sister at thirty-eight; she has no children and her marriage has broken up. Divorce proceedings are in progress, and she is coming home for a month to stay with the mother. The nurse is called Denise and the sister from Australia is Sandra.

Notice that we have possibilities for conflict and tension around one of the most basic of all human emotions: envy.

Think of the themes that most stories deal with: loving, leaving, loss and all the gamut of emotions associated with conflict. Conflict is the natural state of affairs for most of us - even on a small scale. Life is made of opposites, so exploit these abiding interest, as a writer.

Denise and Sandra are going to meet and talk. This introduces the other two elements of a readable story: place and time-span. We have two women who have lived life very differently; each has known a certain type of 'success' and a certain type of 'failure'.

They are going to meet at the bus station at which Sandra is due to arrive as our story begins. This is set in industrial Yorkshire.

The time span of the story is going to be just for the actual ten minutes which covers their conversation in the coffee bar at the bus station.

Note here the choices you have in these three areas of character, setting and time-span:

Character: Age, life history, personality qualities etc.
Setting: Familiar, ordinary, dramatic, exotic etc.
Time-span: The actual time of the events, flashbacks, movement across time etc.

At stage one you have made these decisions and written a summary as above.

Stage Two

Now decide on the sequence of events, statements or stages in the process from A to Z. e.g. it is about a conversation, so how will you develop this? Choices might be:

Rely on dialogue and minimal information about place.

Give lots of atmosphere.

Bring in the wider world, or just their words?

Include inner thoughts and reactions.

Bring in secondary characters?

These decisions are crucial. But let us take the main decision for this workshop of having only the conversation plus some atmosphere. We then need to summarize the sequence on contents:

1. Trivial talks - uneasy.
2. Denise asks how long Sandra is staying.
3. There is a noise outside - roadworks.
4. They raise their voices.
5. Sandra makes derogatory comments about 'filthy, noisy hometown'.
6. They talk about her failed marriage and her lack of children.
7. She raises her voice to say 'I'd give anything for a son!'
8. Traffic noise subsides.
9. In the embarrassment, she could cry, but they both laugh.
10. End with them hugging, wondering why they didn't hug initially.

With this sort of planning, the story will be purposeful, and 'about something' definite if that is what you want.

Stage Three

Now you write the opening section. It might look like this:

Sandra had stepped down from the bus into familiar greyness, her expensive high-heeled shoes landing on dark Grey asphalt. A voice from the past sharply came into her consciousness 'Sandra.... over here ....' 'It was Denise all right. There was the dumpy figure, still a good bit overweight. Motherly, they had always said. 'Now then.... good journey?' 'Ha, you know, so-so. Oz is a hell of a way off... it's not Dewsbury, sis.'

This has done several essential things:
created a mood;
differentiated the two speakers;
given character information (reference to the weight);
added inner reactions;
created contrasts and conflicts immediately.

Final Stage
Write a quick draft of the story. It will probably be about 2,000 words - the average length of most published stories. In that length you can develop a relationship well enough, and add a certain depth of background, mood, physical atmosphere, and so on. Here, you also need to decide on the method of closure. This is a better word to use than ending because in many stories there is no sense of finality. A closure might be an opening out into potential futures. But a successful closure can be done in many different ways. Our story of Sandra and Denise could end in any one of these ways, for instance:

1. They laugh uncontrollably.
2. Sandra weeps and talks about her husband
3. Denise invites her home, not to mothers
4. Denise talks about her fears - she is not Mrs. Wonderful

Genre or not?

This is a fundamental decision, and of great consequence to you as a fiction writer. Do you want to write in a way that is 'free' of any conventions about plotting and planning, or do you want to write a story that sits firmly in a tradition and category?

A genre story means that the plot, characters and language/style all relate to the established conventions of that category: it might be romance, western, thriller, ghost. spy story etc.

The answer to the question depends on how sure you are about why you are writing and how that practice of writing relates to you and your imagination, your past and present reading and viewing, and all other factors to do with the inner power of resources you have which lead you to do something so creative as write fiction.

But some characteristics of genre writing are useful here: Genre story characterized by –

stereotype characters;
situations and relationships which are established in that style of writing;
plot structures, which accord with tradition;
restricted subject-matter and treatment;
limitations in the use of commentary/background/narration technique.

If you write a story which is simply planned and told in a way that suggests itself to you, without any thought of conventions or the way such a story is usually told, that is fine too. But if you want to be published widely, in most cases what readers want is genre fiction. You can write both types, of course.

The difference can be seen most easily in the amount of author-commentary that can be included. Compare these two character descriptions:

1. No real genre:
'Phil was tired of the place. What he most wanted was to get anywhere that was over two hundred miles from Rofton. Rofton was too full of memories. It sounded like Rotten anyway - Rotten Rofton. He wanted out.... out of all these little lives. In this he was no different from you or me. It was that regional thing again, so important to we British. Or should I say English? Phil was as confused as any of us, and I'm telling you his story because he could be you or me'.

2. Genre:
'Phil was the sort of man you notice anywhere. The fact that he was set on leaving Rofton was not apparent. What you saw was confidence, smartness, assurance that he would one day spend time with the winners, not the losers. Jane Millman saw that too, but she didn't want him to see just how appealing he was to her, how much she thought of him'.

No prizes for guessing the genre conventions used in the second paragraph. The point I am making is that you need to keep giving verbal signals to the reader that what they are reading is familiar - in people, plot, setting and style.

Planning and research

As noted earlier, careful planning is usually an important part of success. In the short story, that means both drafting and summarizing. You might begin with character notes or even research notes about places or events. Most planning involves one or all of these:

detailed notes on characters;

experimenting with sequence - putting which event in which place;
working out opening and closure;
deciding what proportion of background to include;
deciding whether to convey the critical information in dialogue, flashback, description etc.

Writing short stories is an activity with no set rules. There is no magical formula that guarantees success. Some writers never plan at all, but carry the story, people and events in their head. Ernest Hemingway often worked straight onto a typewriter. But in most cases, success relates to planning.

The question about gathering ideas, discussed earlier, also becomes important again here. Your filing and logging methods will repay the investment of time now - because when writing, you need to draw on detail. For instance, many types of fiction require a description to be not just:

'Paul wore a black shirt' but: 'Paul wore the black silk shirt that gave him that sophisticated appeal'.

Again, it all depends on why you are writing and for what audience. One of the best things to do as a first step is to read and think about a whole range of stories, published in a variety of anthologies and magazines. Read women's weeklies and also literary reviews. Read small magazines and national ones. Note the differences in the sense of readership and 'house style' and log these details for future use.

****

Chapter 6

Writing a Factual Book

Chapter four dealt with the fundamentals of writing facts. The art of imparting information in a convincing and entertaining way is not easy to learn. It takes preparation and planning. But there is one advantage you will always have over your reader. You will know far more, and so you have every opportunity of making your subject interesting. The reader wants to learn and acquire the knowledge you offer.

Planning
A cursory look at the shelves of your local bookshop will tell you that factual or reference works are some of the steady sellers in today's market. People are aware that we now live in a knowledge-driven society and there is a need for writers who have both knowledge and experience to pass on. Ask yourself, for instance, what factual books you have bought or borrowed in the last two months? Think of the amazing range of possible categories:
biography/autobiography;

instructional;
subject reference;
practical introductions;
textbooks;
hobby guides.

This is just a minimum. Think of all the specialist books on sale and where you find the point of sale outlets. You might be a potential author of a book on keeping gerbils or cats; you might have been a math's teacher for twenty years, or a driving instructor. The list is almost endless.

But this kind of thinking is the starting-point for this category. If you want to write about one of these areas, then this sort of survey is essential. Writing information may be of three basic categories:

1. Established fact: history, geography etc.
2. Mixture of experience and fact : autobiography, instruction etc.
3. Up dating and illustration: reports, statistics, case studies, surveys etc.

You should also consider the groups of readers involved. You need to be sure which group you feel able to write for. These broad groupings are useful at this point:

The general reader
Here, you assume that you can appeal to the browser.
The professional interest
The reader here is someone who has a vested interest. It might be a fellow-academic or someone with a related interest - for instance, a social worker would need to read a book on civil liberties and the law. A teacher would find a guide to school management useful in terms of building on professional expertise.
Defined amateurs
The readership here would be committed interest groups that are involved generally with your subject but want something readable.

Ten Minute Read Culture

In this case, imagine your reader as someone who wants to absorb just the essential facts, and quickly. The commuter, for instance, with a morning train-journey, who wants a language lesson in small segments.

Notice the basic groups here - general and informed. You need to see the reader in your mind and to write a style that is suitable. The best planning is therefore to check on exactly what is needed for your idea to become a book.

This leads to the important stage of writing a summary of what should be covered and how to organize the material. Here is an example, based on a book on Holidays in the USA:

Stage one: Brainstorm

Write every aspect that might potentially be included. e.g. survey of the States, culture and leisure, music, city and country, North and South, climate, historical summary etc.

Stage two- Ranking

Now you organize these into stages of importance. You might do this:

History.
Geographical diversity.
North and South.
Region by Region.
Culture and entertainment.
Hotels and motels.
and so on.

Stage three - Decisions on Scope

Work out the proposed balance - which areas need to most text, illustrations etc.

Style and approach

How to 'pitch' the right style for the intended reader is difficult. But the important decision is what proportion of formality to include. The spectrum of possible styles might be expressed in this way:

1. Formal and factual.

You need to include a fair density of information here. You assume that the reader wants facts, not whimsicalities and anecdotes. It is not a relaxed read.

2. A balance of fun and facts

With this, you plan to include 'rest sentences' - that is, add some elements which are easy on the mind, in between the hard facts.

3. This is an enjoyable read and you'll get the facts too!

In this approach, the reader expects to be entertained. I'm thinking here of the instructional book with lots of cartoons and asides, based on a steady and slow progression. Something like Spanish in One Weekend type of book.

Compare these sentences:

1. French grammar is more difficult to learn than English in many ways. One reason is that nouns all have gender; you have to learn not only the word *maison* for house, but that it is feminine, therefore learning *La maison*.

2. Imagine thinking of everything around you being male, female or neuter? That's what French people have to do from the first time they learn their mother tongue.

Notice the immense difference in the feel of these as you read. Note how there is an attitude behind each one. That attitude is to do with time. The writer has made certain assumptions about how and why the reader has bought the book and wants to learn French.

Writing a factual book involves these considerations. The commercial side counts as well, of course. You need to study the market and see if there is a need, but the professionals will decide that for you, in the end. Just write it first, staging each chapter carefully towards the aim and keep to the boundaries you have set for yourself.

Autobiography/biography
Telling a life-story seems to be the most popular version for beginners. The old saying that every life is a story worth telling comes to mind. But biography illustrates the above issues really well. For example, how would you organize and stage the materials photographs for a life? Your sources might be:

Interviews;
letters and journals;
second-hand opinions;
official documents and records.

So there you are, faced with all this, ready to plan your book. A logic and an order has to be imposed. Do you keep to the familiar format, birth to death, or do you take themes and topics? Do you relate the life to wider background topics? A factual book needs all this pre-planning.

Your preparatory reading
Clearly, what you read affects what you ultimately write. But factual books impose a heavy schedule of reading on you. A positive initial step is to do a literature review. That is, do a survey of what exists and has been written already, but also find out what is actually in print at the moment. Your reading will fall into certain groups, often this is concerned with what exists that is actually up-to-date. A classic example

is a book on beginning photography. The arrival of digital cameras and more sophisticated SLR cameras has meant that some introductory works are out of date. Law is obviously a similar case in point.

Reading might fall into these categories:
1. Densely packed reference- standard works
2. Competitive titles to yours but different in approach.
3. Books on parallel or related topics that impinge on yours.

Sensible methods of research here are to monitor reading in a notebook, keep quotations and references on index-cards or on your computer-database, and most important of all, write abstracts of the really vital topics. You need a friendly reference librarian as well.

Now read the KEY POINTS from chapter six.

****

KEY POINTS FROM CHAPTER SIX

WRITING A FACTUAL BOOK

- Think carefully about what reader you have in mind and practice styles and content boundaries.

- Compare what you have in mind with what exists already.

- Decide on the intended reader and what style is appropriate, especially in the degree of informality/formality you will need in the style and vocabulary.

  - Read widely and relevantly first, and do a literature review of existing knowledge and available texts in your area.

Now turn to Chapter Seven

Chapter 7

Writing For Radio

Although most people who develop an interest in creative writing perhaps associate the term with writing short stories and poetry for the printed page, there has been a noticeable increase in openings for work in the mass media and in performance arts. Now we turn attention to the special demands and satisfactions of writing drama and other creative forms for a radio audience.

Openings and submissions

Radio 3 and Radio 4 are the main outlets for writing in the categories of drama, fiction, poetry and features. There are also sketches, sitcoms etc. but they belong more properly to media studies.

In considering the potential for radio writing, any survey of *Radio Times* will make it clear that there are particular forms and required formats; what must be stressed from the start is that a listening, as opposed to a reading audience quite clearly makes it possible to do quite free and experimental things. But editors need material for the following groupings:

Thirty-minute plays;
one-hour plays;
minute stories;
minute talks and features to 1 hour;
factual profiles/documentaries;
poetry with particular features.

These are clearly very specialist formats, and you need to be a student of the category you want to attempt. Your submissions will be a waste of time unless your writing has these qualities of style:

1. Features which enhance the radio medium.
2. A clear awareness of popular themes
3. A vocabulary pitched at the listener-groups
4. Originality and distinctive 'read aloud' features.

Do a case study
A constructive beginning is to take one type and monitor a week's productions with the following checklist in mind, applied in this case to short stories:

What aspects were particularly suited to radio rather than print?
Did the narrator /voice etc. play an important part?
Was it essential to have more dialogue than in a printed form?
How many characters were involved?
Was the subject matter apparently directed towards a particular age group?

In other words, target examples of what you want to write and put yourself in the place of a listener. You cannot really pretend to do this. You need to be genuinely interested, of course.

Drama
A short dramatic piece, for the beginner, needs to be short and intensively located in one strong theme. The best way to explain is to use an example.

Being Frank A 30-minute play.
Characters: Two men on a cycling holiday (in their forties)
Time: Contemporary
Location: On the road, going to the Lake District

Plot summary.
Frank and Brian are old friends enjoying a break away from their wives and homes.

Frank is a teacher, and we slowly learn that he has something on his mind. He wants to confess something important. The play traces the build-up of his restlessness. The aim is to use the sound effects of the road, and some inner thoughts of the men and their wives at home.

The eventual confession is that in the past, Frank and Brian's wife almost had an affair. This might be a breakdown of the stages and imaginative effects used:

1. Steady opening. Fun.
2. From quiet to busy road.
3. Lunch outside a pub. Talk of the Lakes
4. Brian is a worrier – small talk.
5. Frank almost says something important, in lyrical, serious mood. Stopped by traffic noise
6. In the mountains. Camping. Have a few pints. Talk becomes serious. Frank nearly says something about Diane, Brian's wife. etc.

Sound/imaginative effects:
The thrumming of the cycle wheels constantly in background.
Traffic noise is incessant in all road scenes.
Flashbacks to wives' talk is done with domestic noise - clock, television

etc. Storm noises for final confessional scene.

Technique

In summary, there are three main methods to practice and perfect:

1. Use the atmosphere. Give the listener the sound-picture that envelops each scene.
2. Make dialogue crisp, convincing and appropriate to character.
3. Keep explanatory material to a minimum. Tell, don't show.

An example

This is an extract from the above play:

Frank   Pardon? say that again.... something about Kendal...

Brian   No... mended, I said is it mended, the spoke?

FX Lorry passes. Noise drowns them out. A horn blast then fade out.

Frank.   Hell! Is he just saying hello or is he just insane?

Brian   Mad as a hatter. He'll kill someone. Probably has.

Note these aspects particularly:

A stress on broken, staggered speech, following normality.

A clear pinpointing of what we hear, as opposed to what is spoken

A mix of trivia with a cumulative gathering of character-information.

Stories

Clearly, stories written for radio are partly defined by the time available for the designated slot. The celebrated BBC Morning Story was always exactly 2150 words, but this has been relaxed recently. However, you need to start by writing a story in a simple form. A monologue is recommended. Take one experience and one character, then build up to one significant event such as an accident, a robbery, or simply an important meeting. A useful first attempt exercise is to take the traditional idea of two strangers meeting and one saying something important - or learning something important, that actually changes their life in some way. Your monologue is the one voice reflecting on that formative, significant experience.

For instance, here is a basic idea for a story. A woman of about fifty has left London in haste. She has been stressed-out by the trauma of living in the midst of crime, noise, threats and menace. One day she has just filled a suitcase with essentials, drawn out all her savings, and taken a coach north. Then, on the coach, she meets someone. It is a very ordinary conversation, they part in York and never meet again, but her life has been changed permanently. She has been made to re-think her faith - which she lost ten years earlier on the death of her only brother.

To write this as a monologue for radio, as opposed to print, you need to make the most of these styles:

Go inside her head - be experimental
Play around with the times she refers to
Report conversation either word for word, or summarized
Use sound in both general and specific ways
Contrast past and present

For instance, you could use her inner thoughts to contrast the coach with her former street and neighbors:

There's noise here.... a big engine under us... the walkman tinkling behind, and the old men going on about racing.... but there's noise and there's noise. By God.... when you've had reggae music making your walls bend at two in the morning, you know about noise... I'm not moaning, like, it's just that things like that need to be said. We all close our eyes and maybe our minds these days. Ah, don't mind me... I'm just stressed out. Soon be right again. That's what I though as I sat on that comfy seat.

Note how the ordinary, seemingly disorganized flow of thought allows you to cover any time and to switch easily from three viewpoints. Also, the voice is powerful in its ordinariness. It's never a good idea to be 'literary'. Immediately accessible emotions and sensibilities is the key.

Obviously, as you go on, you can try larger scale stories, but first person narratives based on one intense experience are a manageable way in to this very specialized form of storytelling.

- Keep the key points in mind;
- Vary your sentence-length;
- Use everyday idiom;
- Exploit the sound environment;
- Switch and cut scenes very clearly;
- 'Signpost' changes by sound effects, however simple.

Features
Writing factual pieces for radio can cover anything from social reportage to historical documentaries. With the beginner in mind, the most optimistic and manageable forms are in the short input features for set programs. Supposing there is a regular magazine program that deals with current affairs in a broad sense: something like The Afternoon Shift or Woman's Hour. Monitor the typical contents and find a suitable item. You need to find a subject that is universal, and work on a funny angle or a very informative one, with strong human interest.

A typical example might be a feature on carers. This gives you a range of occupations such as home helps, sitters, care assistants, matrons and so on.

You might go through this process:

1. Advertise for people to interview. Retired people may be only too glad to talk about their careers.
2. Select, interview and record material.
3. Summarize the most dramatic, entertaining and emotive subjects covered.
4. Write up the result as a talk (say five minutes duration)

This is time-consuming, but remember that you are competing with professional journalists and you will do well to achieve even something as short and one-sided as this.

A note on competitions
A very positive move in all radio writing is to start by entering competitions. Check in the Writer's Handbook (see reference section) for details of the Alfred Bradley Bursaries and groups such as Yorkshire Playwrights. The arts associations will also have information on this.

Now read the KEY POINTS from chapter seven.

****

KEY POINTS FROM CHAPTER SEVEN
WRITING FOR RADIO

- Study programs in depth and note contents and styles

- Practice writing from models. Write short pieces first.

- Write short forms, keeping to guidelines on sound effects, single characters and monologue narrative.

- Concentrate on one type of writing at first and plan methodically

- Always follow the main guidelines on target listener and 'house style ' for the program you have pinpointed.

Now turn to Chapter Eight

Chapter 8

Writing Poetry

Clearly, writing poetry is not necessarily every writer's idea of earning a living by the pen. It is very competitive and very few poets earn any money.

The nature of writing poetry is, naturally, related to the expression of emotive and intellectual responses to the world, but it need not be solemn and lacking in humor. This chapter is a short introduction to the art and craft of writing poems.

Can anyone write poetry?

This is a direct and crucially important question to begin with. Writing poetry can stem from various urges and aims, but in most cases people write poems because they have a need to express a strong response. Experts disagree over the answer to this question, but it seems that almost all of us can manage a verse or two of rhymed lines, as in limericks, doggerel and greetings lyrics.

The word poem or the word poetic have been used in so many contexts that the issues are confused. Reviewers will write of poetic symphonies, dances or even watercolors. This can only confuse things in the present case.

As to what exactly constitutes poetry, that is a complex question. However, there is a basic agreement that poetic language and form have these qualities:

A compression of language.

Attractive-sounding language in harmony and in rhythm.

Often uses rhymes or similar devices.

Depends mostly on imaginative style and usage (metaphorical language).

The point is, can you write poetry? If you are reading this section, then you must feel instinctively that you might like to try. In practice, after twenty years of experience in teaching writing classes, I have found very few people who cannot write an adequate lyric. On the other hand, very few of us write exceptionally effective and moving poems to equal the classics. There are some pre-requisites:

You need to be observant.

You need a deep interest in people and how they behave.

You need a sense of inner rhythm - as in song lyrics.

You need to cultivate your imagination.

The more practical side of this involves reading as much poetry as possible, and keeping a poet's notebook.

You write what you read

There has been so much poetry written in English since Chaucer (the Father of English Poetry) in the late fourteenth century that a poet who takes the art seriously needs to read widely and learn from what is read. Consider the fact that, over the centuries until the early years of the present one, most poets have been university/ grammar school educated and therefore had a conception of poetry which related to the classics - to Greek and Latin models.

This is one reason why poetry is associated primarily with rhyme. The classical English poetry used rhyme and metre to copy the models.

71

So what and who should you read?

Reading to learn
Start by reading selections from a large, comprehensive anthology. Note how poetry has changed over the centuries. If you read a sonnet by Shakespeare, then a Victorian love poem, and finally a modern love poem by Roger McGough for instance, you would see changes in all the areas of poetic writing:

vocabulary used (poetic diction);
form and technique;
use of rhyme;
complexity of images.

The most obvious aspect of these is the change in acceptable diction. Now, anything goes: you can use slang, dialect or even obscenity if you have stylistic reasons. But formerly, there were rules and guidelines as to what was a fit subject for poetry.

The more you read, the more you will feel the nature of poetic language. Basically, much modern poetry is an extension of that love of the spoken word we first feel when literature is read aloud to us as children; also, the sheer joy of language as in children's rhymes and songs is part of it. Think about graffiti for instance: something like this:

Einstein rules relatively OK
or
Home rule for Wales
And Moby Dick for King

These scribblings show some of the central poetic qualities of language.

Much of it depends on simple devices such as the pun - a double meaning like Whales/Wales. Think of how many shades of meaning are attached to words such as assurance or tolerance.

Another aspect to note is the way in which poetry renews 'dead' language. Poetry is with us, partly to stop the language from slipping into a moribund state. Verse energizes cliche and truisms.

As you read, also collect the essential reference works: a dictionary, a thesaurus and even a rhyming dictionary if you need one. Bear in mind that you can write a type of poetry within a very wide spectrum. There are hundreds of different styles, approaches and outlets. You might only want to write amusing, satirical, gentle poetry - or you might write serious, philosophical poetry. You may concentrate on only one subject-area such as religious or love lyrics, or even dramatic verse.

You will soon note which poets are there to learn from: you will sense a rapport.

Sometimes a poet writes about the subjects you would potentially explore, and you absorb technique and discourse without realizing it.

Most of all, keep a commonplace book of any lines which exemplify good technique.

The poet W.H.Auden did this, and to read his notes gives an insight into his ideas.

The poet's notebook
Most writers keep a notebook of some kind, but with a poet, it is a particularly constructive habit to acquire. Many use two types: a pocket book and a desk-drafting notebook.

Pocket book: for random jottings based on observation. Keep your awareness of all the language around you sharp and cultivate close

73

listening and reading. Signs, posters, advertisements and conversations are fertile sources of everyday idiom and double-meanings. For instance, you might see a sign in a display-window saying 'Managing Women: A Short Course' Here, managing /man nagging might be the source of a piece of comedy or satire. Note the inventive uses of puns on church noticeboards, for instance. Such statements as 'The highway to Heaven: pay your toll here'

Desk notebook: This is for developing poems from first drafts. You might use a large A4 notebook and write the first draft on the left, then change as you re-write on the right.

Drafting

A manageable first step is to write a prose version of an idea first, and develop this into a short poem such as a haiku. This is an example of a workshop you can do that builds up to a haiku poem.

Poetry may be formal-having a set form- in three different ways:

Syllabic - a certain number of syllables in each line.
Metrical - a certain metre (stress/unstress patterns) in each line.
Accentual- the same number of stressed syllables in each line.

A haiku is a syllabic poem. It has just three lines with a pattern of 5/7/5 syllables:

Under green cover   5
Eyes hide from the morning light   7
We miss their beauty   5

This is a simple descriptive poem from Japanese literature. It just meditates on nature or on everyday observation. In this workshop, you need to use a family photograph album and follow these steps.

Stage one
Choose a photograph having three strong aspects - it might be the person's smile, the location and someone else in the picture.

Stage two
Write a prose description of what you see, using one long sentence for each topic. You might have this:

1. Mary at the seaside- a false smile. She has just been very ill.
2. So the camera lies - the sunny day relates to no 'sun' inside her.
3. The kids play a game of rugby - oblivious.

Stage three
Write the three statements as three lines, as short as possible:

Her smile tells sweet lies
The camera loves content.
And the kids score tries

Notice that you have to work at this. You might have several lines before you find the right one, and you have to play around with words of many syllables and words with only few.

The same kind of approach can be done with all categories of poems, as a first step.

If you want to write metrical poems, the commonest metres in English are as follows:

iambic - unstress-stress, as in the word   unknown
trochaic -   stress-unstress, as in the word never
anapaestic - unstress-unstress-stress, as in the word underpin
dactylic - stress-unstress-unstress, as in the word   perforate
examples of lines in English poetry to match these:
iambic: The curfew tolls the knell of parting day   (Thomas Gray)
trochaic: Never, never, never, never, never.   (Shakespeare)
anapestic: You delayed your serenade
dactylic: Nevermore, nevermore...... (Poe)

Performance

Nowadays, many poets write for performance and for public reading, rather than simply for the printed page. There has been a boom in stand-up and poetry linked in performance, or even in poetry readings given to and by writers' groups. A poet such as Ian MacMillan mixes comedy with poetry, and several freelance writers write poetry for children and work in schools and colleges. You need to decide which is most suitable to your talents.

This introduces the idea of a basic split in our culture between public and private poetry. It is worth recalling that in the distant past, poetry and song were the same thing. But with higher education came the notion of a page poem as opposed to a public recitation or reading. Although we study Chaucer in an intellectual way today, in his own time, he would have read and performed his Canterbury Tales.

There is also a debate about whether song lyrics are poetry. In the Poetry International held in 1996, there was no problem with this. A songwriter like Ray Davies performed alongside 'page poets'. It's words that count; that's what it's all about in the end.

But if you do decide that you want to write for reading and performance, then a careful planning process is needed. You have to work with a group if possible and read as part of a team initially. Regarding the qualities of a performance poem, there are three main aspects to work on:

1. Entertainment through wit, intellectual word play.
2. Use a storyline where possible.
3. Include dramatic and emphatic intonation.

A successful performance poem will set a scene and dramatize, then make one firm, central point. Here is an example:

Lessons

'Dear parents of England,
 Here we hug and burn firecrackers.'
I think of her in a row of dark faces,
beautiful, innocent as a new leaf,
 mouthing the Queen's English or King's Spanish,
the desktops warmed; their classroom frail
but echoing with those nails of power,
 driven in, those words. Like the ones for us.
'We are in good health, here in my house.
Thank the Lord. You are so kind.'
She has freed us from something hard,
 something whose teeth and bones warn us
of the death of love in our cold streets.
We hug and burn firecrackers in Empire Street.

The point about this is that it use two voices: the little girl's from overseas, and the lyric first person 'I'. This gives it a small-scale drama and a point of contrast between two cultural environments.

A performance poet needs to look for subjects with certain communal, social qualities and universal interest, for instance:

political themes;
local stories;
confrontations and conflicts;
satirical commentaries or protest (environment, rights etc.);
ironical stories/sarcasm.

Again, the best first move is to read anthologies of performance poetry and learn from the best. The modern classic volume in this category has to be The Mersey Sound, an anthology containing the work of Roger McGough, Adrian Henri and Brian Patten.

But joining a local writing group is the best practical step. Here you will surely meet other poets, and readings are easily set up. You need to start small-scale, build up both confidence and a tested repertoire of material, and study the best practitioners in action as often as possible.

Now read the KEY POINTS from chapter eight.

****

KEY POINTS FROM CHAPTER EIGHT
WRITING POETRY

- Assess what kind of poet you may be: intellectual, popular, satirical etc.

- Read widely and learn about formal and metrical verse.

- Practice short workshop sessions on easy forms of poem initially, then build up to more complex types.

- Keep two sorts of notebooks: a pocket book for immediate observation and response, and a desk notebook for drafting and working on poems to the final stage.

- Consider readings and performance poetry. Ways of taking poetry out of the study are the modern approaches, and provide more varied outlets for work.

Now turn to Chapter Nine

Chapter 9

The Writers Resource Section

Now is the ideal time to provide a checklist and summary of the resources you have both in you, in terms of expertise and particular skills, and resources available to you more generally. It is intended to be a reference and self-check section.

Skills checklist

You should now be in a position to assess several areas of you as a writer. Write answers to each of these questions under the sub-headings. Then assess and reflect on your answers and responses. This will be a comprehensive guide to your current skills and future potential.

1. *General abilities*

Do you consider yourself to be an efficient reader and researcher? Could you find information quickly for a book-project? Have you set up a personal logging system yet - whether computer-based or simply notebooks? Are you keeping a reading journal or similar log of relevant and preparatory reading? Have you reflected on your interests in popular culture and narratives? Have you expanded your range of interests or become more specialized since starting this book?

2. *Writing skills*

Do you feel comfortable with notions about grammar and usage, style etc? Could you write descriptive notes on any subject now? Do you know how to plan, draft and edit a script? Have you noted your limitations and strengths as a writer? Have you used any reference works yet, as part of a writing project?

3. Your way?

Reflect on any attempts made to pinpoint your best abilities. Have you obtained any feedback yet on anything you have written? What have you learned from the example workshops in this book?

4. Universal resources

Are the writing magazines relevant or useful to you? (inspect one). Have you responded to any adverts about becoming a writer? Do you feel that you work better alone or in a group? Which forms of writing attract you most? (any different ones compared to your aspirations before you read this book?)

Critiques and feedback

If you are serious about writing, and you have been trying some of the exercises in the earlier chapters, you should have some idea now about your particular strengths and aims. What you urgently need is positive and honest feedback. Most writers are familiar with the pointlessness of showing work to friends and family, who usually want to support you so much that they only offer smiles and encouraging noises. You need professional and peer-feedback now, more than ever.

What are the possible sources of constructive feedback? These are the usual ones:

comments from colleagues in writing groups;
correspondence courses - reports and responses;

readings by critical services;
editors' responses.

The problem with most of these is that they cost money. Let's look at each one.

Colleagues
advantages: they are writers like you. they see the good and bad points.
disadvantages: they do not want to offend, and will talk in general terms only.

Correspondence courses
Advantages: Detailed feedback on all work is available, and it is direct and objective.

Disadvantages: Very expensive. You can pay a lot of money on the promise that you will be published by the end of the course - but they can keep extending the course!

Critical services
Advantages: Very thorough and direct. This is professional assessment.
Disadvantages: Expensive. You can pay anything from £30 to 80 for a report of perhaps four to ten sides. (These companies advertise in the writing magazines)

Editors' comments
Advantages: Impartial and by professionals.
Disadvantages: Very brief and very rare. Remember that few editors give you any comments. Usual practice is a curt statement or a rejection slip with no personal comment at all.

Your language: some exercises

The usual areas of 'basic skills' with language are grammar, vocabulary, spelling, sentence structure and punctuation. Bear in mind the need to pick up on any weaknesses immediately. This is a basic list of weaknesses to watch for in your work:

Spelling: Do you have problems with any spellings that conform to a pattern - e.g. double consonants, endings, silent letters etc. If so, there are some guidelines in any standard GCSE textbook.

Punctuation: Are you sure about the proper use of the common punctuation marks - full stop, comma, semi-colon, colon, dash, capital letters, brackets and inverted commas? Again check these terms.

Sentence structure: Just a matter of following three guidelines:

1.Never write unwieldy sentences with too many dependent clauses such as 'He went to see the leader, a man of immense frame; a show -off who played chess constantly and swore; he knew that it was going to be hard.....' etc.

2. Use both short and long sentences.
3. Make it clear what the subject is.

This is a good point to offer you three short warm-up exercises, each on a specific writing skill. Write about 300 words in answer to each brief. Treat this as a test paper.

The aim here is to make you actually write some short tasks and compare your answers to the texts referred to.

1. Description

Write a paragraph about your earliest childhood memory. Build the writing around a scene and bring in details about the objects, smells and sounds around you. Reference text to check: opening page of Cider with Rosie by Laurie Lee.

2. Imagery

Write a poem or piece of lyrical prose about an imaginary experience. Use a dream narrative perhaps, or a vision or daydream. Reference text to check: Seamus Heaney 'North' in Selected Poems (Faber)

3. Monologue

Write a few paragraphs based on a man /woman who is estranged in some way from society -a loner or a tramp for instance. Explain the predicament and refer to his/her past. Reference text to check: Harold Pinter The Caretaker (Methuen) Opening of Act 2.

Working with other writers

All the chapters so far have given the impression that writing is a lonely business, and so it is, for most of us. There is rather too much talk about writing in some writing situations, perhaps, rather than actually creating . But writing circles and groups are invaluable and you should investigate the groups and organization in your area. Your local library will have details, but they are listed in Writing Magazine also. What are the benefits of joining a group?

These are the commonest answers:

discussion and comparison of work;
opportunities for publishing and market knowledge;
criticism and feedback;
possibilities of collaboration on projects;

experience of editing;
learning professional practice;
networking;

Working with other writers might seem too extreme a way to express what is essentially simply a learning process. The group will usually have events and publications planned, and often guest speakers will visit the group and your circle will widen. The benefits of comparing how others work are obvious, but remember that you have to be involved and make a committed effort. Not everyone likes to talk about their writing and many attend to watch and learn.

The most attractive element here is in having some yardstick to judge what you are doing, and how well you are writing. If you meet and listen to others who write what you write (or aspire to write) you may be pleasantly surprised by the value of what you have done.

Workshops

One-off sessions organized by arts associations or colleges are also invaluable. Here, you work in a group, actually writing something in a set time-span. Often these are on one genre or category such as 'Writing Science Fiction' or 'Writing stories for Children'.

Organizations such as the Arvon Foundation run such short courses all the year round, and the relevant reference works are listed at the back of this book.

The real benefit of attending a short course or workshop is that you find out what you can produce under pressure, but there are other specific aspects:

immediate response to what you write;
pressure that may be highly creative;

you work to a deadline;
professionals teach you;
you learn your strengths and weaknesses more quickly;
you learn about one form very intensively.

Monitoring progress
Now it is time to provide a checklist of the various ways of monitoring your work and how you improve - or otherwise. These are all elements of good practice:

1. Your logbook of responses. Keep a record of editor's responses etc.
2. A diary of work done, preserved drafts and any submissions of work to publications.
3. Your commonplace book : any quotations to use or learn from. Put these under categories such as: description: young person/ country scene/ expensive designer-wear etc. Add pictures if needed.
4. An index system for disks or notebooks/files.

As you go on, you will need to keep bibliographies of work read etc. but use this checklist of research sources for each category dealt with in the earlier chapters:

Fiction:
A thesaurus
A good dictionary
Indexes of character/description etc.
model passages/extracts
A stylebook/grammar guide etc.
Poetry
A dictionary of literary terms

A rhyming dictionary
Examples of formal poetry
Markets, addresses of magazines - updated.

Keep addresses of organizations - some are worth joining (the Poetry Society - see the booklist at the back of the book)

Radio:
Stylesheets and handbooks provided by the BBC
Taped examples of model dramas/stories
Information on layout
Lists and examples of 'slots' to write for
Any local/regional outlets

Factual writing:
Reference works on your subject.
A personal index with quotations.
A working bibliography.
A literature review of work done.
An updated index of topics covered.

It is absolutely vital that you always know where your target information is - whether for factual or fictional writing. Start a system and keep rigidly to it at all times. Everyone designs their own.

Now read the KEY POINTS from chapter nine.

****

KEY POINTS FROM CHAPTER NINE
THE WRITER'S RESOURCE SECTION

- Do an honest survey of your basic language skills and your habits as a gatherer of information and material.

- Concentrate on improving any areas of language and expression that need attention.

- Find out about writers' groups and courses and consider them.

- Investigate some of the ways of obtaining honest feedback on your writing.

- Maintain your records of all work done.

Now turn to Chapter Ten

Chapter 10

Submitting Your Work

Although there is a great deal more in my companion volume to this book, Freelance Writing, in which I put the emphasis on writing for publication, it seems sensible to summarize in this final chapter the important aspects of submitting your work for publication.

Covering letter
When you submit an article to the editor of a magazine, you should follow these guidelines:

include a short covering letter;
add a brief summary of your writing successes;
provide material loose-leaf - using only a paper clip;
double space and leave a good margin;
provide a stamped, addressed envelope;

These measures will make it easier for the editor to deal with and read with ease. Never provide large amounts of autobiography or a detailed c.v.

The covering letter should be like this:

Dear Editor,
        Would you please note the enclosed article on macro-photography? I read your publication regularly, and I note that you

have not carried a feature on this for some time.

Although I am not a professional, I have been a member of the.......... group for several years, and I write for their journal, Lens and Focus. I enclose some photocopies of articles I have published.

A stamped, addressed envelope is enclosed.

Yours faithfully,

etc.

Notice that the idea is to show interest, to prove your ability and to indicate the nature of your 'track record' in the area of expertise you offer.

Writer's c.v.

For more prolonged or even book-length work, you will need to have a full curriculum vitae. This should stress your background in three main areas:

1. Educational achievement (main qualifications) and professional activities.
2. Past publications in a related area and other literary achievements
3. Aims and objectives - how this fits in with your central interests as a writer.

This might be an example of layout:

C.V. for J.L. Smith

Education
BA English   Norwich   1976
PGCE   London   1978

Experience in primary and secondary schools:
1980-6   MonoLane Comp. Sheffield.

Publications
Paper on 'Special Needs in the School in a time of Change'   in E.P.S.
Journal Nov.87
Courses/seminars attended
May 88   London   Seminars on Special Needs for teachers.
I have a paper based on above topic.

Current research/writing interests
To produce a handbook for teachers on literary and testing for the 11
year-old age group.

Your aim is to summarize and to stress those areas that relate to your
book/article etc. and not to dwell on minor things. Mention
membership of professional bodies, personal development courses etc.

Presentation
As in all aspects of publishing, the first impression is the major area of
impact. An editor wants to see evidence of these professional standards
in your presented work:

good English. No poor spellings or clerical errors;
clear layout;
readable text;
plenty of attention given to text-size and sub-headings;
a sense of your personality and motivations;
good packaging;
market awareness.

The artistic and creative elements are the most important. Enthusiasm and commitment to the subject in hand are the clear signs of this, and you can easily provide such things. Remember that you don't have to demonstrate too much so that you bore the editor. Finally, show a sense of what reader you have in mind, and everything else will follow.

The c.v. and the covering letter will indicate where your ambitions lie, and also show how long you have been involved in the subject.

Submitting an idea or proposal

If you have an idea for an article or a book, you need to explain in summary form why there is a market for that format and subject in the treatment you suggest.

article:

Suggest a topic indicating length, how you will write it, why it should be suitable for that publication etc. Give a sample page.

book:

You need to produce a substantial document here. The headings would be:

Existing market and need for your book
Competitive titles: what you offer
Summary of chapters
Style and approach
Sample chapter or extract

Now read the KEY POINTS from chapter ten

****

KEY POINTS FROM CHAPTER TEN
SUBMITTING YOUR WORK

- Write short but informative facts and comments

- Give only relevant and related information

- Present material clearly and with user-friendly reading potential

- Supply a short c.v.

- Keep a proposal for a book or article short but densely packed with information

Now turn to chapter eleven

Chapter 11

Courses and Workshops

This is the perfect time to consider your growth as a writer and how you might best develop your skills. At this stage, you will have made decisions about for whom you wish to write, what category or genre you want to write in, and what working methods seem right for you. Thus chapter discusses the option of joining a course or a one-off workshop. This can mean anything from a few modules on an English program or a full-length degree or diploma; it might even involve a master class given by a specialist.

What courses exist for creative writing?
These are the main types of courses:

The adult education class.
This usually involves a fairly loose and chatty group and students write workshop tasks or simply develop their own projects and obtain feedback from the rest of the class. There are not usually any examinations, but in Britain it is possible to gain NVQ qualifications. The emphasis is on informal and fun learning in a welcoming and relaxed atmosphere.

The short course
This is usually on a specified area of writing such as the short story or article writing. It may be on a skill rather than a form, of course, such as developing your plot or writing dialogue.

Correspondence/e-learning/distance learning

These various courses all depend on some kind of correspondence relationship between tutor and student, and your main benefit here is that you have in-depth analysis and feedback on an individual writing project. It can be like a constant seminar! The disadvantage is, of course, that you have no open discussion and variety of comment on your work. It is a lonely business, but then so is writing itself.

A degree course

Writing programs are increasingly popular now, and in case you weren't aware of this, just buy a copy of a literary journal such as Story and you will find dozens of university-based writing courses. It is possible to take a single module focusing on one particular aspect of writing, or to take a wider, full literary studies course, which may even mix writing with other parallel studies such as theory or cultural studies. These often entail the writing of a sustained work as a dissertation piece.

Master class or specialist tuition

In Britain, the Arvon Foundation is typical of this. The student spends a week in one of their three centers, with a group of about fifteen other students and two tutors who are accepted professionals in their field of writing. You would be given writing tasks and deadlines, and close feedback is given. Arvon also have retreat sessions, in which there are no tutors: simply quiet time in which to think and write. In the USA, this is big business, and all the national literary foundations and universities offer similar tuition in summer school programs.

Basically, creative writing is growing as a part of the leisure industry, and more and more institutions are offering short courses under the guidance of well-known tutors.

Why do a course?

Answering this question raises the ancient question of whether or not writing can be taught. Perhaps this is best avoided, and it is more profitable to consider the benefits of such courses in these terms:

They offer guidance, not formulae for instant success.
They might not lead to getting you published, but they give the right advice.
Courses offer a chance for direct feedback on your work.
You have a chance to meet and learn from leaders in the area of writing chosen.
A course forces you to be disciplined and work-directed.

Who teaches these courses?

In most cases, the tutors are full time or part time writers. But of course, many are run by teachers and educationalists. George Bernard Shaw's dictum that 'those who can, do: those who cannot, teach' is grossly unfair but is often quoted. A more reasonable and accurate statement would be from Samuel Johnson: 'I cannot make a table, but I know a good table when I see it.' In other words, it is not necessarily the case that the active practitioners of a genre of writing will be the most effective teachers. A good, experienced teacher may well be far more successful in teaching fiction than a celebrated novelist. Therefore, all you can do is sample a few courses until you find what is right for you.

What can be learnt?

In many cases, successful writers learn their trade simply by persistence, adapting to the market, and absorbing writing skills as they simply build sentence on sentence. Often, these 'track records' are packed with failures, non-starters, drawers full of unpublished work and so on. But then, the same could be said of many successful and widely published writers. We all read about the best sellers that were rejected by scores of publishers before being seen for their success quality.

A reasonable suggestion is to ask yourself who you wish to write for, and a story told by an American writer illustrates this. He asked a group of students who they wanted to write for —the girl reading by candlelight in a tenement, wanting to got to the end of the novel before the light fails, or the rich man with a blanket over his knees, reading your paragraph over and over again? This is certainly a parable about the choice of strong narrative or admirable style. In simple terms, we could talk about writers of type A and B:

Writer A
Writes purely by instinct and has no routine; can only write when there is a story burning to be told; has learned the skills simply by an instinctive grasp of composition. This writer does not read 'the market' or worry about whether people will actually want to read their work.

Writer B
Writes to order; rather than waiting for the muse, he or she asks the muse in for a visit. This type is always studying trends and assessing what has been the formula for success in the books on the current best seller stands in the bookstores. This writer attends all possible conferences, works a lot on the net and insists on being informed about publishers' wants and needs.

It may be that sometimes, being too work-oriented in these terms actually turns out to be counter-productive, and many writers seem to spread themselves too thin, constantly trying to find 'openings' rather than concentrating on one thing. It is useful here to suggest two profiles of people beginning to write, showing certain common characteristics. Which of these two best describes you?

The Frantic Scribbler

He keeps a notebook and seizes on every passing potential idea for a poem or story; enters every available competition and studies adjudicators' reports on previous competitions; writes a whole series of opening chapters and synopses which are sent off to agents or publishers, probing for the right opening. Probably has had some limited success in small literary magazines; not really sure what he should be writing and has no sense of compulsion about writing any specified form or category.

The Focused Natural

He only ever writes one thing – perhaps a short story – and his model is Raymond Carver, the short form professional par excellence. Keeps research notes and writes story ideas and plots in a dedicated notebook. Uses his own experience and that of his family and friends in fictionalized form and professes to have 'no imagination... simply writing from life and telling it like it is...' He has stories fairly regularly in magazines, and on radio. He has a small collection out from a specialist press.

There must be lots of other types, but in my experience, these are very commonly met with on courses and in writing classes of all kinds. All this reflection is here in this chapter because I would like to stress the importance of knowing yourself as the basis of all writing. This sounds trite, but such a simple point is often overlooked by beginner writers. This is because there are many common misconceptions about learning the trade and getting into print, such as:

You have to know someone in the publishing trade.
Your face has to fit.
It all depends on luck.

The best writing is never published until after the author's death. Reading other writers' work stops you finding your own voice.

Much of this comes from the ways in which the writing business is mediated in films, art and literature. Certain myths about authorship still persist, such as the idea that all great authors suffer torments and work through the night in garrets, or that all famous writers have a drink or drugs problem. These are some basic facts to register about the majority of successful writers today: they work hard and see writing as a craft; they have a firm grasp of their typical reader; they remain updated in their knowledge of the market for their kind of writing; they have to lead a very lonely life most days of their working year, and their main ambition is to keep in print, not necessarily to win a Pulitzer prize.

The first step, then, in acquiring a realistic attitude to creative writing is to decide what you want to write and how you intend to work towards an attainable goal. Courses can certainly help you to reach these decisions, but it does take time to locate the right courses, and it usually involves some sacrifices. Today, the Internet and e-mail have opened up an incredible number of new avenues to success, and it is easier than ever before to find the right course for your needs.

Finally, remember than you should know which elements of the writer's craft you need help with. What are some of the things that may be holding back success? It could be your spelling, or it could be that you always rush and never rewrite or draft. In other words, some hurdles are easily overcome; others are fundamental and require a whole new range of working habits from you.

What happens in a workshop?

Supposing you choose not to attend a whole course in writing, but simply do a workshop, or a workshop-based short course. What is meant by a 'workshop'? In most cases, a typical session would go like this:

Phase one
The tutor introduces the theme, method or subject. This might involve general discussion and reading some short examples together.
Phase two
Some stimulus material is presented to the group. This might be photographs or objects, and the intention is to open up universal angles of experience.
Phase three
The students write something, usually a short extract or simply preparatory notes for a poem or story. No one is ever forced to read aloud, of course. It is the individual's choice.
Phase four
Reading and feedback. Members of the group read their pieces and a discussion and feedback session follows.

It may be seen from this example that it is a group learning experience, but the exciting thing about it is that the method of work opens up the random, the unplanned and the individual life-experience of each student. It can become addictive, and there are 'workshop-junkies' of course.

The Importance of Process

Never forget that workshops are about trying out ideas. They are based on the principle of experimentation, and although you will sometimes write on themes directly instigated by the tutor, you will also inevitably find that your imagination quite sharply accesses your own inner pool of quiet waters that is your latent writing. I believe that all writers have the active, restless waters of their daily river of creativity; but they also have this silent pool waiting to be stirred and directed into the river. Sometimes sheer serendipity can do this.

I had a student once who did this in class. I had set the group the task of writing a scene in which someone visits a couple or a family and transforms their life. This lady, within seconds, started to write something. She was totally enraptured by whatever it was that had struck her. When it came to the reading out part of the session, we were transfixed. She had revisited a time when her grandfather had been to see her and her mother, taken then fishing and picnicking, and given them a summer day of utter delight.

This fascination with the process of writing, albeit quirky and intermittent, can be the very thing you need to trigger your real, genuine creative element. In Catherine Cookson's autobiography, Our Kate, she tells the story of going to her workshop with her first fiction in which she had bravely confronted the catharsis she needed in order to transmute her life of trials and pain into compulsive fiction. Catherine recalls that she got a standing ovation from a certain section of the class.

This process is always uncertain, never boring, and guaranteed to provide that delicious hit and miss imaginative impetus all writers need from time to time.

Now read the KEY POINTS from Chapter eleven

****

KEY POINTS FROM CHAPTER ELEVEN
COURSES AND WORKSHOPS

- Study the available range of educational opportunities

- Be very clear about what you need to learn

- Choose the method of learning best suited to you

- Read the reference books first

- Be clear about what a workshop involves

Now turn to chapter twelve

Chapter 12

Professionalism and Organisation

Streamline your attitudes

Now you are at the point at which you should have a clearer idea of what category of writing matches your talents, and what you urgently aim to write. If you have done the right kind of thinking, your have followed your instincts and been guided by such factors as what you love reading, what sort of writing fires your imagination, and so on. Instinct can be a more reliable guide than intellect sometimes.

This is a good time to take stock of attitudes you have developed in the course of reading this book. For instance, have you clear answers to these questions:

Who are you writing for?
What kind of satisfaction does writing give you?
What have you learned regarding technique?
What have you learned from favorite writers?
Do you have a system of monitoring ideas and observations yet?

With these issues in mind, it's time to take a look at how you can move smoothly into absorbing the professional attitudes essential to writing. These are the basic factors indicating your degree of commitment, as professionalism in writing, as in all things, involves a total immersion in your chosen trade, and it has to come first.

The professional writer meets deadlines, keeps to a schedule, obeys the instinct as to when to write, and most of all, actually writes instead of absorbing the habit of talking about writing. The enemies of this professionalism are:

Enjoying the myth of writing – bohemian talk, life in the garret and so on.
Reading about authors and dreaming about joining their ranks.
Being a workshop junkie, only writing when stimulated and never doing much.
Starting and not finishing: the frustration of having huge stores on unsuccessful works – often simply because they were not thought through clearly.

Basic to all these is the exciting, delicious feeling of being carried away by talking about a plot or an idea, just talking around the plot and loving the possibilities of speech. This is what makes the bar room failure: the bore who maybe once knew Hemingway, or who was taught by Mailer. But where is his or her work?

Be professional, then. Go through these guidelines:
Discipline.
Certainty.
Self-Belief.
Confidence in the craft.

Now we look at these in turn.

Reference section
This is a short list of books, magazines and courses that would be helpful to you now that you are starting out as a writer and taking in seriously. If you have finished this book and read all the chapters, you

ought to have a clearer idea now of what you want to write and why - and for whom. You should also know what related information or sources of professional knowledge you also might need.

Books
The two cornerstone reference books for all writers are:

Barry Turner (ed.) *The Writer's Handbook.* Macmillan annual
A & C Black (publishers) *The Writer's and Artist's Yearbook* annual
In addition, the *Dictionary of Literary Terms* by Roger Fowler Routledge) is recommended.

General
J. Fairfax. *Creative Writing.* Elm Tree. 1981
Natalie Goldberg. *Writing Down the Bones.* Shambhala: Boston/London: 1996
J, Hines. *The Way to Write Magazine Articles.* Elm Tree. 1985
Victor Jones. *Creative Writing.* Hodder: London, 1974
G.Lynn Nelson. *Writing and Being.* Luramedia: San Diego, 1994
M. and D. Oliver. *Starting to Write.* How To.1996
Tristine Rainer. *The New Diary.* Putnam, New York: 1978
Miachael C. Smith and Suzanne Greenberg. *Everyday Creative Writing* NTC: Illinois, 1996.
Roger van Oech. *A Whack on the Side of the Head.* Warner, 1990

Fiction
Clare Boylan (ed.) *The Agony and the Ego* Penguin 1993
D. Brande *Becoming a Writer* Macmillan 1992
D. Doubtfire *Creative Writing* Hodder and Stoughton 1993
David Lodge *The Art of Fiction* Penguin1992

Paul Mills *Writing in Action* Routledge1996
Josip Novakovich *Writing Fiction Step by Step* Story Press: Ohio, 1998

Poetry
M. Baldwin *The Way to Write Poetry* Elm Tree 1992
Ted Hughes *Poetry in the Making* Faber 1979
D. Livingstone *Poetry Handbook* Macmillan 1993
Graham Mort *The Experience of Poetry* O.U. 1991
Stephen Wade *Writing and Publishing Poetry* How To 1997

Radio
Giles Cooper *Radio Plays* BBC
W. Ash *The Way to Write Radio Drama* Elm Tree1981

Magazines
Fiction Writer F&W Publications, 1507, Dana Avenue, Cincinnati, 45207
MsLexia, P.O. Box 656, Newcastle upon Tyne, NE99 2XD England
New Writer, PO Box 60, Cranbrook, Kent, TN17 2ZR
The Writer, c/o Kalmbach publishing Co, P.O.Box 986,Waukesha, WI53187-0986
Writing Magazine, PO Box 168, Wellington Street, Leeds, LS1 1RF Yorks., England
Writers' Forum PO Box 3229, Bournemouth, BH1 1ZS

Magazines welcoming contributions
Acumen 6, The Mount, Higher Furzeham, Brixham, South Devon TQ5 8QY England
Lexikon PO Box 754, Stoke on Trent, England ST1 4BU
Literal Latte, 61, East 8th Street, Suite 240-A, NYC 10003

Penniless Press, 100, Waterloo Road, Ashton, Preston, PR2 1EP England

Ploughshares   (non-genre fiction and poetry) Emerson College,100 Beacon Street, Boston MA 02116 USA

Superfluity (poetry) Scribbled publications, PO Box 6234, Nottingham NG2 5EX England.

Websites

General:

HYPERLINK http://www.nawe.co.uk

www.nawe.co.uk

This is the site of the National Association of Writers in Education, UK, and has a directory of writers, details of submissions and abstracts of articles from its magazine, Writing in Education.

Lexicon,

 HYPERLINK http://www.lexikon-publishing.co.uk

http://www.lexikon-publishing.co.uk

HYPERLINK http://www.wordmarket.co.uk

www.wordmarket.co.uk

Connects freelance writers to publishers

HYPERLINK http://www.smallpresspoets.co.uk

www.smallpresspoets.co.uk

HYPERLINK http://www.poetrykit.org/

www.poetrykit.org/

Publishes poems and articles

HYPERLINK mailto:www.guidelinesglobal@inkspot.com
www.guidelinesglobal@inkspot.com
Lists openings and opportunities.

www,wordhoard.co.uk
Information about a growing organizations, with ample scope for
freelances

HYPERLINK http://www.writing.co.uk
www.writing.co.uk
(Internet poets' society)

HYPERLINK http://www.rfh.org.uk/poetry/index.htm
www.rfh.org.uk/poetry/index.htm
(a magazine specializing in utilizing and developing the potential of
hypertext creative writing)

Organizations

Arvon Foundation, Totleigh Barton, Sheepwash, Beaworthy, Devon
EX21 5NS England
Association of Freelance Writers, Sevendale House, 7, Dale Street,
Manchester M1 1JB   England
Book Trust, Book House, 45, East hill, London SW 18 2QZ England
The British Council, 1o, Spring Gardens, London SW1A 2BN
(Has a literature department and published an annual anthology)
Comedy Writers' Association of Great Britain, 61, Parry Road,
Ashmore Park, Wolverhampton, West Midlands, WV1 2PS England.
National Association of Writers' Groups, The Arts Center, Biddick
Lane, Washington, Tyne and Wear NE38 2AB England.

The Poetry Society, 22, Betterton Street, LondonWC2H 9BU England

The Society of Authors, 84, Draycott Gardens, London SW10 9SB

****

PART 2

ACTIVE WRITING

How to use this section

This section is intended to be a practical supplement to the first part of the book. It can be used for individual study or in a class situation. Each workshop represents either a piece of thinking and working done at one sitting, in the peace of your own room, or a distinct class activity.

Levels

The first series of workshops is introductory level. This means that the fiction and factual topics give you the basics of writing. The overall aim is to introduce the range of skills involved in preparing to become a writer and then in maintaining professional and successful attitudes to the process of writing afterwards.

First steps

Creative writing is a mixture of art and skill, sheer hard work and moments of spontaneous creativity .For this reason, this guide makes no assumptions about those awkward words inspiration and creative. In other words, there is a basic belief behind this book that most of us can learn the techniques, just as we might learn carpentry. But having said that, why not also admit that some of us will never peak beyond the journalistic skills of turning an interview into an article, while others will write wonderfully imaginative fiction? To each, his or her own.

Pre-course survey
Please give reasonably full answers to the following questions, as they will form the basis of the tutorial work on the course, and also provide some help for you when you develop a personal action plan as a writer. (Also, look at the Reader Biography at the back of the book)

1. Why do you write / wish to become a writer?
2. What types or categories of writing have you produced in the past?
3. Have you ever submitted work for publication? (please give details)
4. What do you consider to be your areas of interest as a reader?
5. Are there any varieties of writing, which you feel, are not suitable to your skills?
6. Please list and describe any previous courses you have taken that involved an element of creative writing
7. What skills and or knowledge do you hope to gain from this course?
8. Have you recently done any courses or had any occupations that involve writing? (e.g. writing letters, reports, questionnaires etc.)
9. Try to describe and explain your experience in terms of your having had 'material' for use in writing.
10. Have you ever kept a learning diary, or do you log in some way, you're reading?

Preliminary exercise.
1. You will read and reflect on a passage from R.L. Stevenson's essay Random Memories.(See passages at the end of the book).After general discussion, decide on what techniques or aspects of writing style make this appealing (or otherwise) as a piece of autobiography.
2. Feed this back to the class (or write in your notebook if working alone) perhaps writing your conclusions on a large sheet.
3. Write your own opening (400 words) of a piece of autobiography, using this given framework:

An incident or experience from my life:

1. Specific thing that happened
2. Place/ atmosphere/ geography
3. A short snatch of dialogue
4. A national/world event at the time

You should write four paragraphs, each one based on each of these points.

4. Feedback, exchange and compare passages, bearing in mind your thoughts about the Stevenson passage. If working on your own, compare this to any other similar writing. Ignore the late-Victorian formality in Stevenson's prose, and concentrate on the subject. If you are working in a class, ask the tutor to supply a framework for a feedback sheet, as in the example at the back of this book.

LEVEL ONE: INTRODUCTORY

Active Writing Workshop 1. BASIC SKILLS

Phase one:
What skills do I have and what do I need?

Writers need to find out exactly what they have as tools at the beginning of their writing careers. It doesn't matter what stage in your life you choose to take writing seriously. The point is that you want to find out what and if you can write. The 'if' is a small word with a massive protective barrier. It seems to guard those who have succeeded - keep them in a safe enclosure where the real writers live and find sustenance. They have proved they can write, people say. But is there is special formula that can be acquired in order that you may join the successful? Obviously not. But this is a list to start from: write some lists under these headings.

1. Your life-experience
2. Your certificated worth as a language -user
3. Your everyday encounters with words
4. Your reading or viewing.

Phase two
Now you take each topic in turn and look closer. You will be amazed at the potential in each of these areas of imaginative resources.

Life experience: Text: Stephen Wade   Villains and Enemies

Obviously, not everyone is capable of being a constant observer of life. The idea of inspiration (whatever that is) suddenly striking you like a thunderbolt may still be current in some contexts, but the first step as a beginner, needing self-knowledge, is to consider the degree to which you relate to and feel a sense of placement in, life-experience. Questions to ask are these:

Do you take an interest in other people's lives?
How often have you tried to talk to people about their work?
Do you enjoy reading/watching impressions of life similar to yours?
Would you agree that everyone has a story to tell? (Yours is?)
Are you able to list at least three incidents from your life which are 'material'?

Material can mean any angle you wish to place on one incident. Start with one specific event or experience, then write around the sensual and visual data that surround the moment.

e.g. Beach........man on horse riding by....I played, making a sandcastle.......he had only one eye.......called me little champion......I called him Young Lochinvar.....from my favorite poem at school...... one eye but beautiful. Made a drawbridge for the castle...........he could ride in to safety.

Write a similar 'moment capture' and notes on your questions to yourself, for next time. The aim is to keep detail out of the picture at this point, and simply note the outline features of specific experience.

Workshop 2
Phase one: Breaking Moulds

Topic: The most frustrating element in writing - of any kind - is often that you intend to produce something fresh, original, a new way of looking at a subject, and then, on paper, the result is too familiar or it lacks life, and so on.

One approach to escape this straightjacket is to use an unusual viewpoint or play with several viewpoints.

Examples for discussion:
1.The man working on the roof caught sight of the woman out of the corner of his eye. At first it was just a flash of white he was aware of; then he instinctively turned to look across, and it was then he saw her body astride the fence, a red patch growing stealthily in the center of her blouse.

2.The sound of footsteps on the asphalt should have been familiar but was not. They were not Jim's steps. It wasn't time for him to be home, either. She could have looked, but her contact lenses were off, snugly in the case by the bedside.

3. The tiny parcel of clothes in the heart of the forest was slammed and kicked by the wind. Nature had its future in her hands. Limbs wriggled, lungs screamed for help, just to be noticed by someone or something, but there was no pity in that raging storm.

Phase two:

Defamiliarisation
Victor Shklovsky-'Habitualisation devours works, furniture, one's wife, and the fear of war.... And art exists that one may recover the sensation of life; it exists to make one feel things, to make the stony STONY. The purpose of art is to impart the sensation of things as they are perceived and not as they are known.

Exercise: Take the following scene to be used at the opening of a story or novel. You should create a viewpoint that is so different from the norm that we see the scene as somehow strange to us as we read.
As the story begins, there is a man at the wheel of a car. The car is parked in a lay-by in the country. Three police officers are observing the man. They are nervous. They carry firearms. Help is on the way. The road is an arterial route; constant traffic, bright summer day.

You might choose to 'show' the scene in the way that a pilot, an animal, a schoolchild etc. might see it. Or you could make the story emerge as internal thoughts of someone.

Workshop 3
Genres and genre cocktails: Use the Conventions

The first stage of this session is to read together some openings from genre fiction. The class should bring in a selection, reflecting a range of interests.
Discussion points:

What is a genre?
What language uses give clues about the intended genre of a piece?
Can genre writing be as effective as 'serious' fiction as a social commentary or as philosophic, reflective writing?

The group should work around the definition that genre uses a set of accepted codes and conventions which reflect a norm of writing technique. Texts which do not fit easily into genres could be discussed e.g. *Kes, Tom Jones*, Oranges are not the only Fruit etc.

These definitions provide a useful launching pad:
'Genre should be conceived, we think, as a grouping of literary works based, theoretically, upon both an outer and an inner form (attitude, tone, purpose -more crudely, subject and audience 'Rene Wellek *Theory of Literature*

Art develops further until a form is achieved and valued for its own sake...The achievement of form is signaled by a revolution in the ordering of the constituent parts. Elder Olson-*An Outline of Poetic Theory*

Genre cocktails:

The writing exercise for this session is to work on a genre cocktail - a mixture of genre techniques to create a new one. For example, you might interlink a detective narrative with a science fiction, as in the film Blade Runner. Or, discuss and comment on this passage which mixes Philip Marlowe with the gritty northern realism of Barstow or Priestley:

'As I approached the door of my office on the third floor of the Ebenezer Sykes building in Crapley, I knew there was a dame waiting for me - and a dangerous one at that. The perfume lingered on the landing, just beneath the painting of Ebenezer himself, hands in waistcoat pocket, looking complacent.

I tilted my flat cap, put the pipe away, still warm, into my mac pocket, arranged the false smile, and peered around the door. She was blonde, young and lethal. Her legs went right up to where a man should never look, but I looked anyway. It was a day for risks. I'd already bought the Telegraph and spat into the gutter. I was mean as a lawyer without a brief and the world was going to know it.' 'Hi, fella.... you Bill Sidebottom, private Dick?' 'I could be lass, but steady on, I'm feelin' a bit parky. I'll just put this gasfire on,then I'm all yours, flower...'

Workshop 4
Dialogue. All Talk?

In narrative, dialogue can serve several functions:

1. To inform the reader about a character's personality, habits, background etc.
2. To move the events of the plot onwards.

3. To add to descriptive detail

4. To give essential factual information in an interesting way

5. To add variety and interest - it usually gives a sense of realism very quickly

Consider the following and compare them. Each extract comes from the opening of each text. Ask yourself what the notion of 'authentic' dialogue means and what it demands of the writer.

1.After the deluge of sound ceased, after the wind passed, the sailor fell, was sick. They were in a desert of air. 'Goddam! get me out of this,' the sailor shouted. 'Stand up,' the little man said; he began to pull. Crunching sounds came up. 'It's ice' the sailor said. 'Get me out of this.' Falling again, hands became feelers, pawing about. 'I know ice' he said, 'something always moving under ice, I know.' (James Hanley : No Directions)

2.

'All the time the wind was south-west you were deadly keen on seals.' 'Was I?' Allen idly stopped fumbling in the pocket of his coat, then asked with interest: 'Been seeing your friend the boatman again?' 'Yes. Why?' 'This meteorological knowledge'. 'I suppose you think I'm incapable of noticing anything for myself.' 'No.' (Christopher Isherwood: *All the Conspirators*)

3.

'Something a little strange, that's what you notice, that she's not a woman like all the others. She looks fairly young, twenty-five maybe -or a little more, petite face, a little catlike, small turned-up nose. The shape of her face, it's ..more roundish than oval, broad forehead, pronounced cheeks too but then they come down to a point, like with cats.'

'What about her eyes?' 'Clear, pretty sure they're green, half-closed to focus better on the drawing. She looks at her subject: the black panther at the zoo, which was quiet at first, stretched out in its cage.' (Manuel Puig: *Kiss of the Spider-Woman)*

Exercises

1.Write an opening of a story entirely in dialogue, with the speakers discussing something which will clearly show their different personalities.
2.Select the opening page of dialogue at the beginning of a play, then convert this into prose, including all the information, including a description of the scene.
3.Write a short dialogue in which you introduce a specific fact - a statistic or historical information. Make it dramatically interesting.

Note that one fact alone can be of sufficient interest, given the right dramatic situation, emotional velocity, and so on. Every fact does not need to be immediately and deeply relevant to characters, either.

Workshop 5
Writing monologue
Reading Insignificance?

The monologue is perhaps most associated with the art-narrative rather than the popular narrative; that is to say, as a monologue conveys the inner thoughts of a character in an apparently disjointed and digressive way, the reader has to be patient, prepared to accept that to read such narratives is to follow the vagaries of the human mind, in order to achieve something about some universal knowledge of human traits. The great set-pieces of Absurd theatre, such as the close of Act Two of Pinter's The Caretaker, or the intensely realistic method of Alan Bennett's much-acclaimed Talking Heads, show the strengths of this writing as a method of revealing psychological depths.

There are some issues, which are worth considering, though, from the sheer 'mechanics' of writing such styles:

Is it always possible to make the apparently trivial into 'a great theme'? Can interest be sustained by following the ramblings of actual inner thoughts? Does a monologue have to have an element of artifice, or could a real piece of 'speech' written directly from inner thoughts be 'shaped' naturally? How is variety included? Usually by location and other people etc. There are wider stylistic issues to consider also, but the fundamental issue is how to create interest, tension and so on. In other words, is a convincing 'voice' enough to succeed in this form?

Exercises:

1.Read the following extracts from monologues and suggest ways in which the storyline could be changed or developed in order to add more depth or more social commentary-

(a) I was waiting by the bus stop... the one I'd been standing at for the last God knows how many years.... well, this young man had been there, and these two older folk - a man of about fifty and a woman (very smartly dressed) of about, oh, I'd say maybe forty. Well, I'd never said this before cos we hardly ever spoke... in fact never. Only nodded like. Well, this particular morning I said, a bit nervously,

'Mornin', and do you know, their heads turned in shock. The older man actually said to me, 'Do I know you?' That's what he said. Not a word of a lie. 'Do I know you!' Don't that just take the biscuit? That's England for you....

(b) Don't know why I wait here every week for him. He don't care one flea, not a maggot. In fact, do I need the feller in me life? I sometimes wonder. I mean, he'll be round that corner any minute now, frown on his face, miserable as sin, pretending he's not going to touch me for a few quid. For the ruddy horses that is. His beloved nags. He loves 'em more than me.... anybody could see that. But the worm is going to turn, oh yes my lad. Yes me bonny lad. No more easy peezy Sheila in your life. Just you come round there smiling and I might let you off, but I know you're gonna look like a wet Sunday in Bradford..

2. Write a monologue based on one of the following storylines. Write the opening page .

(a) A young woman has left a huge city, packed a suitcase quickly and caught a coach north. She is wrecked by stress, and wants to escape a street of crime, noise and hellish brutality. Next to her is a young man with a walkman plugged into his ears. Write her thoughts as she looks around and wonders whether to speak.....

(b) A man of about twenty-five is walking across town to visit his brother. But this is no ordinary visit. He is deeply in debt after embezzling funds from the Working Men's Club of which he is secretary. He has gambled away thousands of pounds. His younger brother is the only person he knows who has the funds to bale him out. But they haven't spoken for at least two years.... just exchanged polite Christmas cards. Pay a visit to his head and inner thoughts.

121

Further reading:
Alan Bennett *Talking Heads* BBC 1988
Robert Browning *Men and Women* Dent Everyman ed. 1975
Roger Karshner *Working Class Monologues* Dramaline1988
See also audition books for actors which contain a wide variety of monologue forms.

Workshop 6
Factual writing
Categories and Audiences

We now begin the introductory level workshops on writing with a factual basis. This could incorporate any of these forms and conventions:

documentary
feature
instructional
interview/profile
review
opinion/argument/polemic.

The approach is not the first consideration; the first step is to consider the process involved in any writing with a factual element and therefore also with an objective which is to inform the reader. Originality is not an essential component either. As Dr. Johnson said, 'Men more often need to be reminded than informed.' That is, there is always a market for short, informative essays and articles that give important information. The general process will be as follows:

Stage 1.   Consider aims and target reader
Stage 2.   Research the subject well
Stage 3.   Write up notes into a structured piece.

The aims will obviously relate to such purposes as whether you wish to put statement of facts before entertainment, humor, tone and so on. In other words, are you primarily out to persuade, to instruct or to entertain with the facts you have collected? Is the aim to mix some or all of these? Here is a useful exercise to consider some of these things.

You are to write an article for the complete beginner in a subject that you know very well. Choose a hobby or leisure interest for this. Then write a list of what purposes the article might have. Express this in verbs. e.g. To remind, to advise, to recommend, to condemn etc.

Now, select just one of these verbs and write your first paragraph in line with the main intention. For instance, here is an example on the subject of 'Getting into Classical Music' for a general hobbies magazine aimed at young people:

So you maybe never even wondered what a conductor needs to know to use a baton, or whether Mozart really did write the Requiem from a mysterious caller? Maybe you never thought a second about what classical music is all about than the need to tap your toes when you hear the William Tell Overture? Well let me surprise you if you think this is typical of people under twenty. This year's Prom concert's famous Last Night enticed 25,000 people into the Albert Hall who were under the age of twenty. Rap and Jungle are not the only musical forms around.

Your research notes for any projected article should use these headings:

Topic   Style   outlet   readership/audience

Your writer's log should note your preparatory reading in your selected specialist area. For instance, supposing you want to write a piece on school bullying and you have done some interviews and research reading. You have your rough notes ready. What do you do in order to decide on where your submission will go? Use the above headings and read all the education pages of the daily nationals, the weekly magazines and the specialist publications aimed at teachers. The range of tones and styles will tell you where your best chance of success lies.

Exercise:
Choose a specific topic within the subject area of people returning to learn and research the market. Write notes on the potential market for a specified article. Bring your notes to the next session if you are working on a course.

Workshop 7
Textless Histories: From Interview to Article

To set up as a freelance feature/factual writer you could choose to specialize in writing based on interviews and profiles. There is so much 'material' in the lives of people - ordinary or extraordinary. The Oral History movement has been one aspect of this, with historians realizing that articulate people of advanced age can be a kind of 'living history', but in a more journalistic sense, it has to be said that each of us has a story to tell.

Even if you know no shorthand, you can work with a notebook, micro-recorder and typewriter or PC and produce articles about people's lives quite easily, yet in a variety of styles.

124

Consider this example:

Stage one: You find out from a local newspaper that a man is writing his memoirs of the Second World War. Contact him and arrange an interview. Do some market research as to national outlets who would use an article on the anniversary of a battle or, obviously, on Remembrance Day.

Stage two: Use the micro-recorder to have all the words spoken, but put essential headings in your notebook.

Stage three: At your desk, plug in the earphones and play the interview. Write the statements worthy to be used and keep the finger on the pause button!

Stage four: Write up the article.

Of course, this type of writing can cover local magazines and newspapers, right up to specialist publications. The way to make all this easy on yourself is to limit your range; decide on a subject-area, then do these practical record and monitoring methods:

Keep cuttings in a file - topics in your subject range. In an index book (or on disk) keep and update a list of editors and addresses. In a notebook or in a computer file, keep transcripts or summaries of all interviews done. Many could be used later for a different outlet.

Interviewing tips:
Write questions that demand full answers. Begin with 'How far do you think...? and 'Why do you think...?'
Do research on the background of the topic before you begin.

Keep eye contact with the subject and look responsive and attentive.
Set a time limit and keep the subject relevant - but be polite in doing this.

Exercise:
The class first has to decide on a new publication on current/social affairs. Then they act as an editorial board and decide what contributions they wish to invite. A simplified stylesheet could be produced and discussed.

A stylesheet could be written with these headings:
1. Target readership
2. Degree of formality in the vocabulary and syntax.
3. Length and variety of sentences
4. Use of pronouns and extent of quotation.

Interview your neighbor in the class on a chosen topic. Some suggestions are: their experience of school; involvement in leisure/charity work/cultural events etc. Write and ask about ten questions. Then exchange roles. From your rough notes, write an opening paragraph for the publication and stylesheet decided on by the class.

Some opening techniques to practise:
These are some effective ways to begin a factual article –

1. A question.
    e.g. have you ever considered what goes through your mind when you're a copper on the beat at three in the morning?

2. Quote from subject:
     e.g. 'I like to think about the family....or my stamp collection... it
kills time' Constable Smith tells me.

3. Quote from a well-known source:
'A policeman's lot is not a happy one' W.S.Gilbert said.

4. Image:
     Plodding on the beat in the early hours can seem like a guided tour
of eternity.

5. Hyperbole:
     The dogs of Hell can be let loose in Hull at one in the morning
when the drunks start fighting each other, as Constable Smith knows
well.

Additional reading:
Joan Clayton *Interviewing for Journalists* Piatkus
John Hines *The Way to Write Magazine Articles* Elm Tree Books
Ann Hoffmann *Research for Writers* OUP

Workshop 8
Witness to...? I was there!

The word 'documentary' has suggestions of logging, monitoring some
kind of detail, some actuality that will reflect the truth. The modern
television documentary or the traditional documentary film means, for
most people, a prying into life 'as it is lived'. A useful way to approach
this is to consider the idea of a witness to some event. This is the topic
for this workshop. The notion of witnessing something can apply to a

significant event, such as a person who saw a landmark trade union strike or a murder; but it can also be simply social history, such as a midwife in the 1940's who can say interesting things about her professional life before the emergence of the modern medical technology we all take for granted.

These are some possibilities for the potential 'recipe' to include in documentary writing:

Dramatic, intense first person accounts
Straight historical data
Letters, journals, diaries etc.
Statistics

Notice that these imply a specific way of handling information, depending on your target audience or purpose. Suppose, for example, you want to write an article based on some statistics about education. You find some basic statistics about a local further education college, such as the fact that maybe very few people from ethnic minorities attend Access courses (courses equivalent to 'A' level for mature students). You discover that over the last ten years, only 2% of students on these courses have been from such minority groups.

What possible documentary treatments of the subject are possible? You could find students who are attending language classes locally and talk to them. Find the cultural, social and religious reasons why they do not go on to Access courses. Or you could relate the local facts to national trends. Then find potential markets in the press or in educational magazines.

What does a documentary style mean?
A famous definition from John Grierson, the founder of the British

documentary film, is the 'imaginative interpretation of actuality'. Here is an approach that means taking people doing or saying interesting things about human experience and letting them speak for themselves - but not totally. You edit, select and arrange what they say by providing a commentary for the reader.

Exercise:
Choose an occupation that is unusual - one that you know very little about and write a list of questions you would ask a person who does that job. (e.g. undertaker, novelist, advertising agency work etc.) Direct your questions towards a particular 'angle' on that job such as sensation, curiosity, humor, sarcasm and so on.. Then write an article based on imagined answers. In other words, it could read almost like fiction. After that, try out the real thing. Arrange an interview with such a person and try the approach and viewpoint. The difference between the two versions will highlight what real documentary writing is about.

Further study and practice:
(a) Find articles in the New Statesman weekly that are concerned with documentary investigation. List the styles/ techniques used to give a sense of realism and actuality.
(b) Add to this a checklist of how the material has been interpreted for the reader.

Further reading:
Christopher Dobson *The Freelance Journalist* Butterworth Heinemann
Paul Mills *Writing in Action* Routledge

Workshop 9
Introducing....Your Guide To

A particularly useful and manageable form to write in when starting out as a factual writer is the informative guide to any subject you care to mention. People do not seem to mind reading about Feng Shui, wine or American Football for the twentieth time. There are some things in life, which always seem to provoke curiosity, and we like to be informed.

Consider the various ways of putting across information on any subject.

1. The facts. Literal, direct and relying on statistics etc.
2. A personal angle. The day you tried to understand chess or squash and went to learn.
3. The A-Z guide. Here you can present established facts, sourced from a reference book or from an expert, in a chatty, readable way.
4. You interview the expert and take things word for word.

Each approach has its own advantages, of course. But before you practice these and decide which suits you best, let's have a look at some short examples of what not to do when it comes to presenting facts: these are extracts from a range of articles. Note down what you feel is the weakness in each case.

1. Photography is an expensive mistress. Devote your time to her and you will be forever haunting shops and drooling over the gear you can't afford. You will buy every glossy magazine you see, and imagine yourself as a millionaire, stocking up on the latest models of automatic cameras. But it need not be like this. You need to decide early on what is your type of photography and stick to what is needed. You might need a lightmeter, a fish-eye lens, a cable release. Who knows?

2. Consider all the facts you need at your fingertips to take up a small business. Just think of the contacts you will need. The experts, the experienced. Where will you find them, and can you trust them? Have you realized how important such things are? But you have started to read this, having bought this magazine, and that is a bright start.

3. Bodybuilding need not require a massive investment in equipment. You do not have to re-vamp your garage and turn it into a gym. There are other ways of getting fit. But spend a while simply assessing your needs as you aspire to a peak of physical rightness. You need to be attuned to your body, to eat properly, to somehow see your body as a machine and as a spiritual, individual organ, part of you, your self, your being-in -the -world. Then turn thoughts to muscle structure and blood pressure, body mass and heart rate. Maybe (1) is fine until the last mind-boggling sentence? (2)   is disorganized. The reader would be confused all the way here. (3) Commits the sin of bombarding with jargon.

Exercise.
The secret of this kind of writing is to plan and structure well before you write. Try this short exercise. Imagine that you are writing a handbook on a subject you know well. Decide on the chapter headings and list these, then write a checklist of the information that a beginner would need, in order of importance, as a basis for a first, introductory chapter. Your rationale for this should be based on a sensible and user-friendly breakdown of the material you intend to cover, staged for progressive use, with recaps of factual information.
Workshop 10
Reviewing the Situation

A Form Open to All?

In theory, anyone could sit down and write a review, providing that he or she has a basic ability to express ideas and responses clearly and with interest. We all must have taken part in a discussion about a book a play or a film and then realized that someone made us see things another way, opened up other avenues of understanding about art.

But things are not so simple. To write a review of a text in a set number of words is a challenge to a writer that entails a specific set of disciplines. A cursory reading of The Writers' Handbook would perhaps give the impression that magazines and journals are always looking out for freelance reviews, but this is not so uncomplicated as it may seem. However, a constructive first step is to consider what the function of a review is. (I will use book reviews in my examples, for the sake of ease and consistency):

To inform the reader about value
To give an educated opinion about style and content
To introduce readers to a quality writer
To enthuse about a personal favorite

It might seem that a review is a personal indulgence - a chance to express the reviewer's opinions and taste. Yet, a proper reading of the books pages in Sunday supplements should make it clear that a good review does several useful things. It can give compact information about the author, highlight the strengths of a style, indicate what additions to existing knowledge are in the text, and so on. Having said this, it is still possible to allow a reviewer space to indulge personal, highly individuated readings, but these are rare. The length is also a crucial factor. Imagine the constraints on the writer who is asked to review a detailed, academic work in only 300 words. Equally, journals such as The Times Literary Supplement may sometimes allow a length of 3,000 words if the subject is deemed to be significant enough.

With these aspects of the craft in mind, what are the essential requirements in style and treatment of the subject? Here are some suggestions:

1. Knowledge - based on close reading or on the wider context
2. Personal experience. For instance, in most cases, the reviewer has relevant experience that lends some depth to the writing.
3. Related publications. Obviously, editors like specialists to review in most cases.
4. Entertainment with information. It should be, above all else, readable. Potentially, a review is a mini-essay, with weight in its own right. The writer can easily provide an interpretation of a book's central argument or plot.

Examples of approaches:
Here are some common approaches to the problem of how to review:

The authoritarian -I know more than the writer. My review will make this clear to all my readers.
The dilettante - I am not an expert as the author is, and sheer energy and gushing praise will fill the page well enough.
The sceptic-Do we really need another book on Dickens? There's nothing worth writing about here. Try again. Maybe I could do better, but I have better things to do.
The academic -I shall weigh and consider, perhaps confusing you even more with the weight of my learning. But by God, you will feel that you have learned something.

Exercise

Write notes on the effectiveness of these styles to reviewing. Which would you find most appealing to the general reader? Assume these are all from weekly newspapers covering books for non-specialists.

1. Novels like this are rare as white rhinos. And when you do find such a treasure, enjoy it, relish it, take your time. I was sorry to reach the last page of this adventure yarn - a tale well in the tradition of Kipling or Rider Haggard.

2. If you like your stories plain and direct - and actually about something you can recognize as real life, then stay away from this novel. You will feel a numbness in the brain after three pages. No help is offered, and you cry out for footnotes or even translations at times.

3. The author's three previous books dealt with the northern states of Italy in the Renaissance. This makes a new departure, but the themes are still there - loss, parting and isolation in woman's lot. But the Feminism is only there in the people and the dialogue, never thrust at you like an essential therapy to cure your narrow mind.

****

Level: Advanced. Introduction

Again, the handbook is organized into workshops covering both factual and fictional writing, but now the material is more demanding, ambitious and innovative. The aim now is to give full rein to your own skills and natural tastes in language use. Much of the material here relates to subjects who are often discussed in specialist short courses, but again, I want to simply introduce a range of approaches.

After completing the workshops at the introductory level, you should have some idea now of what style, genre and format suits your talents and aims and therefore you could concentrate on the topics at advanced level which relate to work already done.

Before starting this next stage, however, it will pay to consider once more the points about each individual writer's aims. Do you have more idea now about your potential expertise, your necessary decisions about what to write and why? These questions are worth some thought at this point:

1. Does 'getting into print' seem to be a priority for you, or does learning skills matter more, regardless of time available?
2. Do you feel confident enough to submit a piece of writing to an editor now?

Think about the reasons behind your answer.

3. Have you read consistently in the area in which you want to publish - and therefore do you feel confident that you 'know the market' as well knowing the style, conventions, and so on?
4. Have you considered reading your work to anyone for a constructive criticism, before submitting it for publication?

5.Do you feel fully aware of what re-reading and editing involves?

If any of these questions are impossible to answer, then check in the A-Z of technique in part three of this book. It is all really a case of knowing which tasks are essential and which are optional. The fact is that authors now are asked to do quite a lot of the work previously done by publishers, and these means that as a writer, you need more skills than simply writing sentences and building up to novels or biographies.

Fiction
Workshop 1
Making an impression
More than one way to........

The easiest habit to acquire in writing fiction is to give the facts of a scene or person just as they appear to the eye. This can be effective, of course, and simplicity often presents something to the reader that is becoming less easy to find in the current climate of experimental writing. But what the Impressionist painters did for landscape you can do for your fictional world -with some practice. Reflect on these descriptions:

1.On the pillion, John felt the air whipping at his ears as Gray pushed the machine on to the ton. They were tearing up Beacroft hill like bullets. John's heart was in his mouth. But he daren't say a word. Gray yelled and screamed with the joy of it. John gritted his teeth and tried to keep his dinner in his belly.

2.Cold air lashing the ears. A grinding, churning rumble underneath between his legs. John shook with a nameless fear. The road came up to meet his gaping wonder as the tinny, rattling plates of metal around that thrumming engine pulsed excitement into his veins.

The first only differs significantly from the second in that it is more distant, less concerned with the actual sensations of experiencing the bike-ride. The reader sees John as in a documentary, in a sense, observing all details as they are drawn and examined. The second is impressionistic, in that the reader feels the sensations more directly. The writer needs to find words to describe the feelings. sensual responses and visual shapings of the experience itself.

For this reason, impressionistic writing often makes use of some useful techniques:

Using sentences without subjects;
Cutting out explanatory adverbs and adjectives where needed;
Positioning the reader so that one angle of view or feeling is given;

In other words, the aim is to make explanation minimal. Consider six things that could be said about a building. It could be tall, brown, old, without windows, on a hill and exposed to noise of a nearby motorway. You could give all these details in the orthodox way, building the information gradually to 'set the scene' like an establishing shot in a film. Or, with a sense of perspective, you could present just one angle to the reader. Maybe something like this:

You felt dizzy squinting to look up to the heights of the windowless block of stone; dizzy because something about the plod up the crumbling steps made you want to keep an eye on what was above, feeling like a warrior expecting a defense of the walls he was about to storm.

This simply misses out a large amount of normal description and expected data. It also places the reader in a position that demands thought and adjustment, seeing the narrative from a viewpoint, which asks for some attention and challenges a few stereotypes of descriptive writing.

All that is needed is some thought about the ways in which the best impressionistic writers go to work. Some interesting examples are provided by the short stories of Katherine Mansfield and Anton Chekhov. In their stories, the reader often feels an immediate contact with the perspective needed. In Chekhov's story, The Swedish Match, for instance, we have:

The window had a gloomy, ominous air. A faded green curtain covered it. One corner of the curtain was slightly turned back, which mad it possible to peep into the bedroom.

This is so simple, so minimal, yet it invites a view, a stance on the part of the reader.

Exercises:

1.Try to write an interchange of dialogue in which the reader is made to feel a sense of 'overhearing' the talk.

2.Convey a scene by building on the effects of a storm or tempest, but seen from the point of view of something non-human.

Workshop 2
Following the flow
Stream of Consciousness

This phrase, 'stream of consciousness' is used to convey a sense of a narrative giving a full sense of all-inclusive experience - the whole spectrum of experience rather than an ordered, selected discourse with a logic provided by the writer. The easiest way to understand this is to reflect on your own inner thoughts that float in and out of your mind all day, while you are automatically doing other things.

To appreciate the effect of this style as it was first written in the Modernist period of the 1920s, it is necessary to explain how the idea of realism is normally perceived. When a text is referred to as 'realistic', often what is meant is that there is a semblance of the way in which the narrative relates to identifiable experience. But all the verbal effects are carefully crafted in order to achieve this sense. What seems real may be simply a well-researched piece of description, for instance when a poet who has never been involved in a war writes a seemingly realistic war poem. (Ted Hughes' poem Six Young Men comes to mind).

Stream of consciousness seeks to delve deeper, even more so than a monologue, as discussed earlier. This is an example - an opening of a fiction in which a man is defined and expressed through inner thoughts:

And so I was that I saw the ghost of my father - well, not really a ghost as such. I sensed him didn't I? Did I? I always feel like this when I go back to this place.... nothing here to remind anyone that this used to be a proper community.... there was a pig-sty there.... and a grocer's on that corner. I wanna be your man... Can't get that blasted tune out of my head..... Fireweed..... I remember fireweed everywhere here.. and rhubarb.....fields of the stuff......

There are several pitfalls inherent in this, of course, however flexible it may be as a method of revealing character and mood:

Disorganization. The reader still needs a compass, a sense of direction
Distraction. A mind revealed in this way may seem trivialized to the point of obsessive, irrational behavior.
Obscurity. This demands a great deal of the reader, who tries to understand a personal inner world.

So what guidelines are useful for this adventurous and imaginative style? There are two important ones. First, if you write short fiction, there is no need for methodically developed sub-plots. As a short story method, the stream of consciousness demands an intense expression of one inner world. Second, if used as part of a longer fiction, as in much of Virginia Woolf's novels, then you need to help the reader a little by writing about a focused, limited area of experience or locale.

The best way to learn the strengths of this approach is to read a number of texts, and maybe for most of us, a mixture of this method with others is the most viable compromise if you can't take on a full-scale fictional form in this manner.

For instance, in Christopher Isherwood's first novel, All the Conspirators (1928) this method is used briefly, interspersed with the main text. In his preface to the 1976 edition, Isherwood saw his mistakes and made this comment:

'I now detect a great deal of aggression in this type of obscurity. Young writers are apt to employ it as a secret language which is intelligible only to their friends, the members of their group...'

In other words, following the 'flow' of thought in its randomness and whimsicality is still intended, still part of an overall design, and the trick is to make it seem not to be so. Isherwood was honest in expressing the view that he was not happy with his attempt to do that.

Exercises:

1.Write a passage of narrative in which a range of responses to a single stimulus to mental association is given. (e.g. A gift given to someone which brings the past to mind)

2.Write a sensuous, visual account of a place using at least six types of detail, all seen by one person, thinking at random.

140

Workshop 3
Symbolic Orders
Making things stand for other things?

As Polonius said in Hamlet, we find directions by 'indirections'. That is, language points to other words and concepts. All imagistic language will open out to provoke ideas and images in the reader's mind. As a writer of fiction, you will obviously think in images much of the time. But a symbol is a special image with an extraordinary power if used well.

A symbol is a central image, one that suggests a whole range of related ideas. Where an image such as a greyhound compared to speed suggests only one thing - speed of movement, a symbol connotes: it offers several possibilities. For example, here is a symbol used in the opening of a story:

'The great towering offices of Sol Associates marked the way to everywhere - the future, the past, success, failure and more. It was everything about Brownsville that Joe Soap would know. People looked up at its metallic platings, its iron walls and its glassy towers'.

This building could be used and re-used as the story progresses. Each time it is referred to, the same bundle of connotations are urged into the reader's mind, and then further connotations will develop. This is why a single symbol in one line can be so effective: Dave stood in the lift, the grille pulled across him. Just like my life, he thought.

Used in the first way, as a recurrent, dominating image, it can dictate the themes of a whole novel. E.M.Forster is fond of this technique. The heavens and clouds in A Passage to India or the elm in Howard's End. Of course, Forster makes the tree suggest the permanence and

141

persistence of a vanishing England, a land with a soul and a poetry, under threat from a wave of philistinism. With restraint, such an accumulation of detail around an image can provide some real depth. Take a simple object such as a photograph, and build around it, so that a simple physical description becomes something strongly poetic:

'She held the fading yellow-tinged photo and her hand shook. It was a beach scene, like so many from the post-war years of Kodak Brownies, ice creams and cricket on the sand at Scarborough or Filey. It was an image of happiness sullied by a relentless force that had greedily eaten away at everything good, everything fine..... the five faces were barely recognizable. But she couldn't take her eyes away. There was something magnetically compulsive about this snap. The present had been eclipsed by it - blurred and ochre though it might have been, chewed by time's jaws'.

Notice that the trap here is in accumulating too much detail, layering so much around the central symbol that a directness is lost. But there are some aspects of symbolic writing that provide helpful indications of a sensible application of the technique:

1. Make the image concrete and simply expressive.
2. Avoid cliche and stereotypes.
3. Keep the symbolic elements short
4. If using them as Forster does (as a leitmotif), hint rather than provide discursive accounts of meaning.

Again, it is in reading and noting the best uses that success lies. Perhaps one of the most impressive classic examples is in Thomas Hardy's account of Egdon Heath at the opening of The Return of the Native, where we have this: 'The qualifications which frequently invest the facade of a prison with far more dignity than is found in the facade of a palace double its size lent to this heath a sublimity.........Haggard Egdon appealed to a subtler and scarcer instinct, to a more recently learned emotion than that which responds to the sort of beauty called charming and fair....'

Hardy gives several aspects of an inanimate, timeless place in terms of the almost human. It can symbolize a hundred things to a hundred readers.

Exercises:
1. Take a well-known and overused image such as a knife through the heart or a heart of iron, and transform it into something new, suggesting particular emotions or thoughts.
2. Choose one of the following and place it in a description of a town or city in such a way that it represents certain things:

An ocean liner, a Rolls Royce, a young horse, a steam engine.

Workshop 4
A sense of reality
Realism

The idea of a piece of writing being real, as discussed in the last workshop, concerns the methods adopted in order to present the reader with a sense that somehow the story gives a sense of identifiably recognizable experience or data about an agreed interpretation of reality. The stream of consciousness approach admits that there are as many 'realities' as there are selves to define and respond to them. But the traditional idea of realism is interesting to an aspiring fiction-writer. Harold Pinter provides a neat way into the topic. In his account of explaining how his so-called absurd plays depicted character, he talked of the pretence, in the 'well-made play' that characters give a verifiable account of who they are.

Pinter was provoking his readers to think about the subtle ways in which a sense of realism is constructed by a skilful artist. The main techniques are soon monitored:

Use of dialogue with slang, dialect, local colour
Intense descriptive processes, with adjectives and adverbs used profusely
Background detail and factual research
Use of sources e.g. photos or painting as the basis of visual description
Information that is of its period etc.
Use of genre conventions

It is no difficult task to bring examples to mind: the poets of the First World War provide a typical case. When a writer wants to show war in all its horrors, he or she has a ready-made topic - some area of knowledge that is well defined, and that the reader probably has no first -hand knowledge of. The war in the trenches had a vocabulary of its own, a social setting, a defined, unique landscape, a mix of classes and types, no real literary history in terms of genre, and so on. In other words, the writing of that period from the front was soon described as realistic. As Owen famously said, 'My subject is War, and the pity of War. The poetry is in the pity.' (Preface to Poems)

But in the sense that most writers want their fiction to seem real, there are more practical matters. For instance, the distinction between genre and non-genre fiction becomes important in this context. In genre fiction, it may be that a brief filling-in of acceptable setting, physical objects and so on will be enough to suggest this; whereas in non-genre writing there may be a demand for detailed, accurate data relating to period and people. This is easily seen in the western.

Examine this passage from a western novel:

'Mary looked at the floor, then busied herself with washing the crockery and cleaning the table. Joe walked out on the porch to smoke a cigar and watch the last hues of orange on the plain as the sun set. He loved this place. He knew every crack and splinter of the Double Ring - buildings, men, steers, everything His father had built the place single-handed since he rode into Texas with a drive from back east'.

This could be easily written by anyone who had never been to Texas - or anywhere in the USA. Could the same be said of a modern classic such as A Fistful of Dollars? In the opening paragraph of that novel these words are used:

Sombrero, poncho, reins, boots, spurs, mule

It may be that even in that very successful novel, there is little to verify a real knowledge of the place, period and son on. If you read a non-genre novel, of course you would still be aware of the sense of how the writers knows the subject, but there is a breadth and a pace, together with a freedom from narrative conventions which allow for much more of a sense of reality to be drawn. But this does not always happen. Compare Ian McEwan's *The Comfort of Strangers* with Graham Swift's *Waterland* to see just what differences may be made in terms of how a sense of reality is given. McEwan writes about Venice without naming the place, and makes it convincing even in a short novella; Swift writes a long novel set in the fens, and makes it so discursive that he even includes a chapter on the natural history of the eel.

So perhaps there is no real difference in the sense of reality conveyed in fiction, regardless of the type or category? It may be than it is in the degree of sentimentality given or suggested, but this is hard to make clear-cut.

What are the best techniques to learn, then, in such an array of possibilities? It all comes down to these considerations:

1. How do you make your factual data /research come across without being boring or intrusive?
2. What makes dialogue effective?
3. If the topic dealt with is secondary knowledge for me, how can I ensure a sense of reality?

The answers to all these questions are in the degree to which you have absorbed the required language and idiom. The historical novel gives a useful instance of this. In some such fictions, a huge amount of historical knowledge is evident, and the reader has a sense of the text being factional - a mix of fact and fiction (Robert Graves' *Claudius* novels come to mind). Yet in others, a few deft details give enough flavor for an authentic atmosphere to be conveyed, as in many military fictions.

But in most fiction involving a factual or informative basis to the plot, the writer has to assume an existing interest in the reader for these matters. Bernard Cornwell's *Sharp* novels contain incredibly detailed knowledge of rifles and small arms. Cornwell knows that people who buy such novels also buy historical texts.

Exercises:

1.Practise-using research notes in fiction, by researching the life of a famous person and then writing 1,000 words, which fictionalize an event in his/her life.

2.Compare and contrast two genre fictions in terms of an analysis of these elements:

Use of slang/idiom
Location/setting
Authenticity of dialogue

Workshop 5
Tales and tellers
Metafiction

The theories behind such issues as who tells the story, why and how, easily fill the pages of whole libraries of an abstract pursuit called narratology. For the literary scholar, there are depths of enquiry concerned with how a writer uses narrative technique which are rewarding, and open up new readings of texts, but for the writer interested in the skills behind such storytelling, it is the practicalities which matter.

However, once you start to write with more subtlety and awareness of stylistic devices, some innovative possibilities occur. For instance, if you note how a novel such as Wuthering Heights tells its story with the help of several narrators and various time-references, then your awareness of the sheer power of such processes is increased. Note, for instance, that the well-tried approach of the author's voice being present in the narrative has an interesting pedigree. Henry Fielding, in

Tom Jones (1749) inserts essays into the novel, at the beginning of each chapter, so that the voice and tone of the writer is included in the storytelling.

Fielding's ploy is a version of metafiction, which is a term applied to the modernist writer's tendency to break down boundaries between what is fiction and what is 'life' outside that fictional discourse. Charlotte Bronte's appeal to the reader is a part of this. You as the reader are made aware that what you read is a fabulation, something constructed to tell such a story in such a manner. Metafiction is therefore as much about storytelling as about the plot itself - or it may be about the author-reader relationship. These tend to be the varieties available to you:

1. The use of yourself as a 'character'
2. Yourself as a voice, a commentator on the story
3. Your angle on events as a way of relating to the reader
4. A general awareness that this structure of words forming your story is a game, a shared experience of imagination and playfulness.

The question arises - why do these things? In a sense, metafictional styles are a way of helping comic or even philosophic themes to be expressed. The approach is ideally suited to such fiction. The 'Our hero' stance is typical of this, in film reviews and similar discourses about narratives. But there is another reason. Such a device enables the writer to swiftly overcome time reference problems, logical structures, development of sub-plots and so on. That is, metafiction lets you take full control and write with a certain all-pervasive power and control. It is as relaxed as a pub raconteur, assured of the audience present. The tone creates the story and the interest.

If this is totally new to you, then here is an example for your study - and your opinion:

'So Roy went away from the interview a wrecked man Squashed, destroyed. He knew then that he would never make it in management. Was it the gift of the gab he lacked? Did he have no charm? Or was it that his face just didn't fit somehow? A thousand unanswerable questions raced through his tired mind as he paced the corridor towards the lift. And you would, wouldn't you? I mean, I did when I failed interviews. And, believe me, I failed plenty. You know the feeling too - well do, dammit. We're all human. So think about Roy at that moment. A guy with five kids and a mortgage - oh, and a nervous quivering of the wrist, which was then worse than ever, as he waited for that damned slow lift and some privacy at last'.

The comic novel in recent decades has invaded metafictional territory, and as you read such passages as the above, you notice the similarities to the 'stand-up' routine and tone of voice. Clearly, this style lends itself to introspection, digression and a jokey, flexible humor. The difficulties arrive when writers try to intellectualize matters by using such styles.

What are the advantages of metafiction for serious-comic fiction? Some ideas are that (a) the writer can write directly, free of formal restraints and (b) it enables the writer to keep contact with the reader, making the whole imaginative process interactive, in a way. A few lines from Fielding can illustrate this:

The reader will perhaps imagine, the sensations which now arose in Jones to have been so sweet and delicious, that they would rather tend to produce a cheerful serenity in the mind, than any of those dangerous effects which we have mentioned.

Notice the careful elaboration of a slow, gentle, wordy tone that makes the whole enterprise of reading the novel a pleasant one. Whether such devices are possible now is arguable. But certainly, one challenge is to try to write a story using the second person singular pronoun - you. As a comedian tells a story, so you write with the reader directly addressed. It is difficult to maintain this, but could be done in a short, mainly impressionistic piece:

'You know the situation, you want a toilet. It's dark, it's one a.m. You've had a skinful of weak lager. You shiver. No public convenience in sight. What do you do? You ask a policeman, of course, just like you're told, as a little boy. So, you do.'
This is a real challenge to keep going and to add structure and incident. But it can be done.

Exercises:
1. Write a metafictional version of a story that exists in third person. Select one character and treat that character as the one of metafictional interest for the reader (as Fielding does in Tom Jones)
2. Create a character-profile and write the facts about the person as a curriculum vitae. Then integrate these facts into a two-page story, with a commentary by yourself about the opinions of people who knew the person - as mentioned in the c.v.

Workshop 6
Questions of Vocabulary
The Right Words?

A recurring problem in writing fiction is the question of the basic language used. If you imagine a series of language styles and registers along this spectrum, think how many different ways there are of creating that writer-reader relationship:

1. Formal, precise, bookish ------------------------------- Slangy,easy, 'talk'

In other words, the words, which make up the attitude of the writer to the subject are selected, often intuitively, from a vast storehouse (langue in linguistics)which comprises the entirety of the components that constitute the English language. An interesting way to highlight this is to place one word that jars into a context. Can you spot the offending word here?

'John knew that he had some time to kill. He could hang out with the guys from the club, or just talk football endlessly till he yawned inside to his brother Paul. But, no, this was the morning for loitering around the Our Price store. Just handling the vinyl and listening to a few things, just letting time settle easy and slow, that's all he could handle just then'
.

The answer could be several words. Maybe you noticed 'loitering'-formal, too old-hat. Or maybe you found other give-Away's. It would be an easy task if you're eighteen, as this was written by a man in his forties who hadn't absorbed the right register - the write language in exact context - for the setting involved.

The point has been made by many editors of fiction lists. A fiction writer has to have some of these instincts for the right words, and right means appropriate for the reader-writer sharing of the subject. The tone created by the writer is particularly important in the short story, in which a rapport, an immediate understanding, has to be established well and efficiently. The wrong word will demolish the best intentions.

What factors need to be considered so that you will get it right?

1 Characterization. Research into authentic talk is essential.
2.Intonation and pronunciation.   The words in dialogue have to be resonant and entirely convincing.
3.Descriptive setting - this should be delineated neatly, not in depth, or it gives the effect of artificiality, a straining for effect.

Learning from the masters

Raymond Chandler used to keep a notebook, and this records his interests and methods. He noted occupational slang and technical terms, but also precise descriptive language such as these lines on 'Fashion notes - men'

:

' Gazelle leather sports coat nutmeg brown. Coconut straw hat deep beige with pugaree band. Light tweed jacket with dark buttons.....' and so on.

Slang was his specialty, and he realized that a writer of fiction needed to fill in detail for the reader in crime stories, as there was a vicarious pleasure involved. The reader, safe in the comfortable free world, for instance, would be intrigued by prison slang:

'Beak	Judge
Buried	Held incommunicado
Broom	Disappear hastily'

Metaphorical vocabulary- how far should you go?

Words always cry out to have full exercise, to extend themselves in the fluency of a narrative into their furthest capability towards imaginative expression. How does a metaphor remain natural and integral to the language in the context? For instance, if all writers tried, as Oscar Wilde did, to create memorable and exaggerated images such as:

'Ignorance is like a delicate exotic fruit: touch it and the bloom is gone' then the stylistic problem would be that all imagery was there to raise the eyebrows or cause a smile. Chandler himself made artificial metaphors for detective fiction that sends itself up: 'She sat in front of her princess dresser trying to paint the suitcases out from under her eyes'.

Guidelines
The answer to these issues lies in keeping to the integrity and belief you have in the unreality of your fictional world and how it relates to the actuality you have in mind as a source - or even the unreality you have in mind, if you write about the planet Mars as Ben Bova does, or Terry Pratchett and his *Discworld.*

These might be helpful pointers:

1.Trust your 'ear' for authentic words in context.
2.Keep notebooks and also recall the way in which words are spoken (intonation)
3.Learn from contemporaries - and from other popular narratives - keeping a check on neologisms - words created for a new concept or purpose, such as Cyberspace or Nerd. Always note changes of usage within certain age groups and within fictional genres.

Exercises:
1.Record a scene from a radio or television soap or drama. Then play it several times, noting words under age-group categories of the speakers.

Study the differences and also the proportion of vocabulary under these categories:

(a) Slang (b) dialect (c) Contracted forms (d) Cliches (e) Striking images

2.Write a character-sketch in which one character is trying to talk in an idiom which is unfamiliar - e.g. when someone goes away to college and is among speakers of a different variety of English, or an older person trying to talk to young people at a family party. Make it seem like the opening of a story dealing with 'The Outsider' theme.

****

Factual Writing: Advanced

Workshop 1
Giving Instructions
Readers want to know how.

It was Dr. Johnson who said that people more often need to be reminded than informed, but, although that may be true generally, we live now in an information-driven society and people want skills - sometimes for sheer survival. One type of writing that always seems to be in demand somewhere is the category that gives minimum but readable advice and instructions on skills and practical knowledge.

A simple piece of market research in this area is to do a survey of the shelves in local bookshops and libraries under the subjects of law and self-help. These are always full of new series or new concepts in shortcuts to knowledge, or texts offering help in finding your way through professional jargon and procedure. Knowledge is power. It's that simple. We all know it, but few ever gain enough expertise in one area to have the confidence to tell others.

Telling others is the key here, combined with an ability to simplify and summarize information. But there are traps. Here are some caveats:

1. Never be pompous. Write an accessible style.
2. Do not use technical terms without neat explanations.
3. Use 'white space' - that is, give thought to layout
4. Cover only a set amount of knowledge and never digress.

On top of all this, there are some stylistic features that need to be practiced, mainly in terms of vocabulary. Here are some examples to try, in order to see whether you have the language skills for this.

Warm-up exercises

(a)Explain a technical term in a way that a layperson could easily understand, e.g. Literature review (from a book on How to do research). A literature review is a summary of what work has already been done on the subject you wish to enquire into. It might cover books, articles in journals or even computer-based information sources. Try your own. Think of an abstract word which you could explain at length, but limit yourself to fifty words.

(b) Making the abstract concrete:

So many difficult concepts are expressed in long words. Instructional writing involves turning these into examples or instances, or even into plain English. Try a common one such as the idea of 'off-side' in football or 'the judiciary' in law. Again, use fewer than fifty words.

Developing an idea

If you want to take such writing seriously, then you need to go through this process in preparation :

Stage 1. Write a list of the subjects you have knowledge about, or which you could write about with some preparation, interviewing etc.

Stage 2. Decide on the one with the most potential, then see what articles, magazines, books etc. exist already. Is there a need for one on your topic. You will find this is common sense. There should be dozens available on , for instance, starting your own business, but how many will there be on organizing a quiz league or starting a philatelic club? Is there a market?

Stage 3.Study magazines and professional or amateur publications, however obscure these might be.

Stage 4.Write an article for a magazine on a well-defined area. If it's on collecting needlework samplers, then choose a period or a style.

Layout

The layout is essential in this category of writing. You need to use headings and sub-headings, break down the information into small manageable portions and use plenty of lists. You might draft out a plan like this, based on the subject of learning to use a particular skill in photography:

Macro shots (close-ups) - lenses, subjects, light factors, most suitable subjects, classic examples - working by themes.

That simple jotting has a scheme to it, a structure that can be developed into headings and given a logical progression from A to Z, which is what a beginner needs.

Exercise:

Research and write a proposal to an imaginary publisher for a new handbook on a 'How to' theme. The length should be only 20,000 words, with the beginner in mind. Use headings, give the topics of each chapter and say who might buy such a book.

Workshop 2

Reportage

Hard and Straight- you tell it

Reportage is a genre pitched somewhere between documentary and autobiography. A recent anthology, edited by Geoff Barton, has chapter headings covering 'Eye-witnesses', Journalism and journalists', 'Death Row' and so on. There are some hints here as to what the term actually means. Social documentary accelerated might be a phrase that comes near to defining it. Geoff Barton points out that it is mainly about the process of reporting, and this is helpful.

In essence, this process is a self-conscious affair. If you want to write this, then you need a presence, a personality, an aura of importance mixed with sensitivity. The topics tend to be politicized in the widest sense - about power and powerlessness and about the act of seeing this. It may be seen as a version of writing which 'reports on today' and always with an eye to injustice and the need for change and provocation. Writing this type of journalism means that your audience should learn about something way beyond their everyday experience, yet with an injection of sensationalism.

Consider this example:

Thief-watching:
'I had been packing goods into cardboard boxes and tying them with string for about a week when I first saw Mitch nick a woman's dress. Mitch was out to buck the system, hit the bosses' wallets, get anything that might be snatched, and generally not sweat   hard to make ends meet. He was a little wiry Scot with a dynamism in every joint and nerve. He'd seen the inside of a few of Her Majesty's penal institutions and liked a skin full of ale once a week.

But on this Friday afternoon, after a liquid lunch, he felt the need to take his wife a 'wee gifty hame'. He took a very small pink dress into the toilet with him, and emerged some time later, beaming with triumph. He pulled his shirt open and there was the pink underneath.
'Wraps round me real sweet like....reckon I'll get somthin' outta the wifey toneet, you ken wha' I mean?'   He winked. 'They'll frisk you man!' someone teased him amid the general laughter.

But they never did. Rumor had it that he ran a market stall with the stuff he shifted from the store.

Notice here these features:

1. An immediacy
2. Plenty of slang and matching tone of informality
3. Minimal visual description
4. A stress on action, not passivity or depth of enquiry.

The aim is for an immediate effect which will relate (a) to the validity and interest of a personal witness and at the same time (b) suggest a wider reference, perhaps to a social issue or something timeless, human, philosophical.

It is helpful to see the drafting of an article in this category, so here is a summary of the process of writing, based on an article on 'Sitters' - people who sit with the terminally ill.

Stage one:
Notes on physical atmosphere - representative words - emotive vocabulary (cancer)- silence - night work - isolation - age of clients - some very young.

Stage two:
Select lines for use in dialogue passages, based on interviews (maybe a composite, based on interviews with several people)
Stage three:
Play with several openings - one with speech, one with atmosphere etc.
Stage four- list topics in order:
Scene
story about 'first death'
children dying
sitter's own experience of illness

how she keeps objective
final dialogue.

It often pays, as with all writing , to study the dramatic openings of reportage by the best practitioners of the genre. For instance, the opening of The Detective by James Mills:

'Looking south into the chaos of his precinct, Barrett says, 'this is a fast track, and if you can't stay in the ball game you get farmed out. If you're a little old lady detective, you end up in a little old lady precinct.....'

Notice how the man speaks for himself, and that the style is reliant on the vibrancy of the real language - the occupational slang. Raymond Chandler used to collect specific slang and keep them in his notebooks for use in his 'hard-boiled' fiction. There is a similarity between Chandler's genre and reportage conventions.

Exercise:
Write a short article (400 words) on any experience you have had or witnessed which was either dangerous in itself or indicative of a threat to social harmony and order. (A riot? Demonstration? Theft? Criminal damage to property?)

Workshop 3
The essay revived
Columns of Opinions
In the heyday of the English essay - the years of the Georgian belle-lettres, when Chesterton, Belloc, Lowndes and Lucas flourished there was a huge demand for short essays exploring anything, as J. B. Priestley

put it, 'from philosophy to lamb chops'. The word essay suggests a painful task undergone at school in which we were asked to discuss rather solemn subjects. But ever since the Spectator from Addison and Steele in the early years of the eighteenth century, there has been a firm tradition of essay writing in English literature.

Now, the vestiges of this once popular journalistic-literary forms in the hands of learned amateurs are to be found in the writings of professional journalists or celebrities such as Alan Coren and Keith Waterhouse. What chance does the novice writer have of making a mark here? If you think in terms of a national market, then very little, but start small and local and you might succeed.

After all, there is a noticeable expansion now of outlets in magazines - most of which cater for the browsers who are looking for something manageable for coffee-break reading. The features of the column or essay-article are humor, first person and contemporary feel. The style needs to be approachable, chatty but with a sense of the writer being actually informed and up-to-date.

Perhaps the secret of success in this form is to be found in the conventions and established tones of address from writer to reader. There are some common strategies, which seem to do well in this context:

1. Take a current issue and send it up.
2. Use irony - very English and gentle but effective.
3. Celebrate English eccentricity and confusion in the face of modernity.

In other words, the conventions of the form are based on certain stereotype aspects of Englishness. Dr. Johnson's Rambler essays exemplify this, and Priestley's even more so. These openings will illustrate the most important feature, though; that of direct curiosity and firm opinions:

'It 's Sunday afternoon preferably before the war. The wife is already asleep in the armchair and the children have been sent out for a nice long walk. You put your feet up on the sofa, settle your spectacles on your nose, and open The News of the World.'.
George Orwell *Decline of the English Murder.*

'...There was once a time when merely wearing long trousers brought me delight. In those days, when I must have been about fifteen, I had only one suit -my best - with long trousers.'
J.B.Priestley. *Long Trousers.*

'...It is recorded of some eastern monarch, that he kept an officer in his house whose employment it was to remind him of his mortality, by calling out every morning at a stated hour,' Remember, Prince, that thou shalt die.'

Samuel Johnson   Rambler 17   *Contemplation of Death*

Note the use of drama, anecdote and a close, direct and confident style, a certain tone of curiosity and a feeling of setting out a stall for a sales pitch, as it were.

As with all categories of writing, the essay-article needs some craftsman's labor. You need to cultivate a character, a specific voice and identity, and to talk around the subject, drawing references from anywhere or anything to hand. Use a notebook, copy quotes and summaries of events and stories under headings for future use. Decide on the subjects that are going to come under your range of interests and keep to them.

Exercise:

Choose a current issue in the news. Find three references for inclusion in your article - a story, a fact and a personal experience, then write three openings, using each one, check on which is most effective, then develop the piece into a 600 word argument. For instance, the topic might be physical punishment in school. You might use: A story from your own school experience; a reference to a scene in Tom Brown's Schooldays and some statistics about vandalism and order in schools in a particular area -use information from the publication Social Trends for the latter.

Workshop 4
Travel writing
Been and seen?

On the face of it, any holidaymaker with a sense of enterprise should be able to write a travel article. After all, they were there and millions of casual readers of magazines were not. Equally, those who stay at home should have an equal advantage over those who live elsewhere. If you live in Majorca, you have ready-made readers in Wigan or Leeds. But it is very difficult to find print as a travel-writer. There are plenty of people working at it, and although the weekend papers are crammed with short articles about decent and attractive venues for next year's holiday, there are few openings for the amateur or the unknown.

However, all writers but the few lucky ones or geniuses have to start somewhere, and you should start in the local paper, the free supplements, local radio and so on. The first step is to choose your category. It could be argued that travel writing now has settled into these established types:

1. The reflective, laid-back tour for food-lovers and sun-worshippers.
2. The adventure playground - aimed at the young or young-at-heart.
3. Real adventure - travel to exotic and distant parts where the water is dodgy and the natives not always friendly.
4. Specialist travel - culture, bird-watching etc.

In addition, there is the chatty type of writing that falls somewhere between travel and column, but overall, which one of these is you? They all involve research of course, from books and people as well as the visit to the locale itself. You need a mixture of facts, personal reminiscence and human interest. There are probably too many styles to choose from, but it is easier to say what should not be done rather than give a magic formula. Here are some too predictable or dull approaches:

1. The heavily informative. This has too much historical or topographical information. The reader will respond by finding a library-book instead.
2. The indulgent. 'My friends and I played cards all night' lines of chat will suggest either trivia or boredom.
3. The Lawrence of Arabia traveler. Don't make it sound as if the likelihood of suffering is very high and that you are appealing for masochists.
4. Sun and sand. There has to be something more. Snippets, anecdotes, local flavor etc.

Travel writing lends itself to a really anecdotal style. These openings will hint at the potential range open to you:

'When in Valletta, don't miss the harbor trip to see the ports and be told about the minesweeping days of the last war. Strong stomachs essential'.

'Toronto appeals to all types, but most startlingly to those in search of the United States without the bragging'.

'Mevagissey left nothing to be desired as long as you desired just calm water and long drinks on the waterfront'.

'We sat in the canoe for three hours and there was just water, water everywhere, the sound of loons, blue sky and singing from the occasional campsite on the distant shores of the lake'.

In other words, if you are a failed novelist, then this could be the form for you. If you really want to write autobiography, then this is one way into that. Travel writing is capacious, allows self-indulgence and lets you lecture with a sense of importance, as you are addressing those with no knowledge. You have been and seen. You can talk with authority then? To an extent, yes. But the secret is to express your personality generously mixed with some reliable information and not a little glamour or exoticism.

The tradition of developing a personal style, which appeals to anyone who likes a good chat, is never really under threat. Humor is a bonus here, and it's always worth a try. But if you are not naturally a comedian in your prose style, it is safer to rely on the occasional quotation from those witty travelers who have been before. You might write with Noel Coward's memorable style of saying 'Very flat.... Holland.' Say the obvious, and make it an occasional joke.

In the end, the hard fact is that editors of national papers and magazines want their contributors to have published already. So write something for a local outlet and stay in these areas: (a) A direct reflection on a trip to a place that is a little different from the norm (b) A piece based on an interview with someone who has traveled to a very unusual place.

Exercises:
1. Write about your own town or village for a publication meant for foreigners (The European perhaps?)
2. Draft out some notes on a recent holiday and send a synopsis and opening paragraphs to the local radio or newspaper. there may be a short 'slot' which is suitable, but editors will want to know a little about what you can do and who you are first of all.
As always, study the best contemporary examples, not necessarily the very literary ones. Eric Newby is perhaps one of the best models here: a master of humor and anecdote.

Workshop 5
Write what you know
On Your Doorstep

I once met a student teacher who needed to do a project, but she had a small family and not much money. Other students on her course were doing fieldtrips and hiring landrovers. Her solution was to study the flora and fauna of her back garden.

The academic paper was excellent and gained her a high mark - quite as impressive as the work done by the travelers. There is a lot to learn here about freelance writing in general.

The old adage about writing only what you know might not be right for everyone, but the principle behind it has some sound advice. After all, writing itself is largely a matter of developing an attractive and suitable style on a subject, the heard work being done with pen and paper, or PC and screen. The writer could do worse than pry into some local subjects first and work towards a column in the local paper. These are some of the potential areas of work:

1. Local history. This might involve any of the following approaches: oral history and interviewing of residents, study of archives and local publication or political writing.
2. Recreation and hobbies.   A column on films, gardening, fitness, sport and so on might be a way towards your first publication.
3. Campaigning for an issue - perhaps an environmental or health topic that has a current significance.
4. Reviewing - arts, books etc.
5. Entertainment and humor. This might even be in local dialect. Many local papers have a column for dialect writing or comic memories and stories.

The procedure is as follows:
Stage one: Ask some basic and direct questions of yourself - what do you know about and what do you take a genuine interest in? My local evening paper has columns on gardening, films, local bands, fishing and community news. All these have openings for amateurs and freelancers to a certain extent.
Stage two: Research your subject and make it a current issue, perhaps

something relating to national news. This might involve interviewing a local expert.

Stage three: Draft out a version of a short article - say 700 words. Make the piece lively, containing your own 'mark' or voice. Include some factual content to show that it's not just 'off the top of your head' and would be better on the letters page. Include a covering letter with some basic information about yourself.

Read a range of local publications - usually available in your library - and discover what exists. My area is reflected in a display cabinet in the local library that contains:

poetry booklets;
a literary magazine;
an autobiography of a man who fought in the allied landings in Italy;
local history publications;
Museum publications.

Whatever you decide, just be sure that you are taking something on which is genuinely you. Here is a case study to illustrate the point:

Fred Richardson wanted to write for the local paper. He had written poetry but now fancied himself as a writer on local history. The factual research did not interest him; what he wanted was to write memoirs. He set about writing notes on a whole group of small villages around the town. He was seventy, and had worked around the area all his life, doing a really broad range of jobs. He had a thousand stories to tell, and the column he established became a real success. He had found an 'angle' and it was on something he knew, by instinct and by temperament.

Exercise:
Survey a local paper, and note what subjects are not covered. Draft out a plan for an article on something you know well. Research at least six facts - statistics etc. - and include these in the draft. Send this with a covering letter to your local editor.

Workshop 6
Autobiography
A Book in all of us?

It has been noticeable in recent years that there has been a growth of small press publishers who have produced autobiographies. The subjects tend to be war memoirs, strong human-interest topics and unusual, eccentric people's lives. One local publisher, Yorkshire Arts Circus, has made a specialty out of such things, taking ordinary lives as the basis of a publishing program which reveals the lives of housewives in years gone by, work in various industries and even community studies or sport.

Having a life that should be interesting and publishable is not necessarily a guarantee of success, though. It has to be written, and written very well indeed to catch the eye of even a small publisher. It may be that there has now been a glut of such writing in the sense of the main categories such as war, growing up in deprived areas and so on. As in all such cases of a glut, the genre has to be opened out in order to prosper. That is, writing about those areas of life which have not been given adequate attention is more and more necessary if you want to succeed.

Given that most autobiographies of people who do not happen to be celebrities are focused on notions of witnessing world events or living lives of great hardship, what will increase your chances of success?

Maybe some possibilities are:

1. Writing about the ordinary from an unexpected viewpoint, such as the young man who realized that all accounts of life in a comprehensive school had been written by teachers, so he set about writing the student's eye view. He observed the everyday events and mixed them with drama and national or generally significant events.
2. An identification of the life-experiences as being 'significant' in some way. Classic examples would be Christie Brown's My Left Foot or Eric Lomax's The Railway Man.
3. Strikingly unusual human interest - a really irresistible viewpoint on especially emotive subjects. Stories of triumph in adversity seldom fail to capture attention. Recent attempts in this vein have been the account of how a prostitute eventually found a new life through degree-study or the autobiography of a nurse, written when she was ninety years old, thus providing a rare memoir of the development of a whole profession from one witness to change.

It may be observed from this checklist that there is always something new, just when publishers and readers have the feeling that all versions of autobiography have been written, something radically new comes along. Imagine the initial impact of Laurie Lee's Cider with Rosie when it first appeared in 1959 and the impact of that opening paragraph:

I was set down from the carrier's cart at the age of three; and there with a sense of bewilderment and terror my life in the village began.

Considered in the light of a genre of village memoirs in which the emphasis had always been on nostalgia, documented facts and the struggle for regional identity, Lee had added a great deal more, and it's not all sentiment, which is a tendency of that species of autobiography. It is, in fact, wonderfully poetic.

It appears to be the arresting, appealing style that increases the chance of success in this as in so many genres and categories of writing. But what can be borne in mind in this particular context?

First, the need for accuracy and honesty. Second, a strong 'angle' or human-interest subject treated directly. Thirdly, a universal statement of a life with experience that would always appeal to any reader.

Exercise:
Use your family photographs to put together a mini-account of your life, done as a simple chronology. Then extract at least three incidents that would form the framework for a short biography. Write this first as an article, based on one strong central story concerning yourself or a relative. Use this as the basis for further enquiry. The development work might involve interviewing and recording other people of course.

Pre-Course Survey: Comments on the Questions

Why do you wish to write?
The point to consider here is your basic reason – do you need to write? Are you primarily interested in somehow writing out your own problems and concerns, or do you wish to communicate something to others – with urgency and importance? Perhaps you simply want to entertain or to provide your reader with 'escapes' fro reality?
You're previous writing.
Consider what you have written before this course and why you wrote it. Have you only ever written 'to order' as part of a course, such as GCSE? Perhaps you write a diary or a journal, or maybe you write letters. All this is valuable is assessing your main needs and interests as a potential creative writer.

Publication

For some people, publication is the main objective. However, if you have ever submitted work to an editor, then this raises the subject of feedback and criticism. Obtaining information about your writing in this way is a long and slow way to learn about your strengths and weaknesses. Other possibilities might be, after completing this course, to use a critical service. For a small fee, you can submit writing for professional comment. Only use the organizations who advertise in reputable writing magazines, however, such as Writing and The New Writer (see the reference section).

Reading

Consider the idea that what you read with passionate interest will be the text you write well. In other words, think about how and why you read. If you read biographies or factual books in preference to fiction, what does this tell you about your involvement in narratives and what you want to gain from the reading? Think about your habits as a reader – what genres and categories you most often buy, borrow or browse. Many writers start by writing derivative versions of their favorites, and then develop their own style within the category.

Writing which does not suit you.

First you have to know your skills. This is perhaps the best reason for doing a writing course. This is because you need to know which of the basic skills you do best: characterization, plotting, dialogue, description, imagery and so on. You only learn by doing. If your answer is a certain one, indicating that you know what you write best or least successfully, then you have already learned something valuable.

This is for your tutor. He or she needs to know what you have done before as there may be established pre-conceptions in your mind about this type of course.

Sit down and honestly ask yourself what skills you want. If you have written basic things such as 'writing good sentences' or 'understanding plotting' then you have a basis from which to move on.

Other writing.

This is intended to ask you to reflect on writing that you have done which may not be 'creative' but may show you that certain fundamental skills you have already acquired have a place in the creativity you have in you. For instance, you may have to write reports in the course of your occupation. What forms and structures, and what type of reader-awareness does this demand? These questions help you to understand how all writing has a lot of expertise in common, regardless of how imaginative it might be.

'Material' for writing.

This is about the nature of your subject as a writer. If you have written down some examples here, you may have listed things from life-experience which are potentially interesting as writing material. The question is intended to open up the class discussion about what is or is not an accessible domain of raw data for writing. The question also implies the research and preparation issue. That is, how do you access the raw material? Suppose you have been in the army for five years and you want to use this experience in your writing. You would need to have a knowledge of what is already in print, what is simply stereotype and what readers want to know about such experience which they can only perceive vicariously.

Diaries and logs.

If you are a diary-keeper or you have written learning logs for previous courses in any subject, you will have opinions about the value of this reflection. There are certainly many examples of writers who used detailed diary-entries as the basis of their fiction. Christopher Isherwood, for instance, worked in this way. A reading log, even if made up of random notes, may still be a fruitful basis, a resource for writing applications. The point is whether or not you have enjoyed this – or have you seen the writing here as a chore?

****

PART 3
REFERENCE

A - Z of Technique

This checklist is intended to provide you with the minimum guidelines for clear and exact, expressive writing. The points are simply 'golden rules'.

Accuracy. Always re-read for accurate expression and facts.

Brevity. Be brief and concise wherever possible. Beware of long, tortuous sentences with too many subordinate clauses.

Clarity. Say precisely what you mean. Ask someone to read your typescript and if they do not understand any sentence, then rewrite!

Digression. The only place where digressions might pay off is on comic writing.

Endings. In fiction, these are not always dramatic and radical. Check stories by Hemingway or Mansfield to see how open-ended stories can be as effective as those which are neatly finished and complete.

Facts. In fiction, use sparingly; in non-fiction, make every fact earn its place.

Genre. A type or category of writing, e.g. crime splits into detective, whodunnit and so on.

Grammar. Know the grammatical rules, so that when you break them, it's for a particular stylistic effect. (e.g. Raymond Chandler: 'When I split an infinitive, it stays split'.)

For basic grammatical knowledge, see Graham King's Good Grammar in One Hour (Mandarin, 1993)

175

Hyperbole. This is exaggerated expression, as in I must have told you a thousand times. This is very effective in humor at times, but should be avoided in most cases. Again, ask yourself how the reader will respond.

Irony. This is very difficult to define. Basically, it means that a writer's real

meaning and intention is different from the stated or implied one. The easiest way to see its use in fiction is to read Conrad's use of the narrator, Marlow, in Heart of Darkness. Here, his story has several levels of working and application.

Jokes. In factual writing, obviously, a good story that illustrates the topic will some effect that will help page-turning quality, but use sparingly and with a sense of the context and character in fiction.

Kinetic. Meaning a narrative with a reliance on action. Of course, things happen in stories, but one of the most common traps for beginners setting out to write fiction is that lots of things have to happen. Not true at all.

Linking. A simple word for a real craft. On its simplest level, this means linking sentences and ideas clearly and relevantly. For instance, do not always use the conjunctions, and, but, then, so. Linking on a more sophisticated level is about joining the events in a story or poem seamlessly. Use cuts, as in films, or place events together for dramatic effect. (juxtaposition). The main guideline is do not tell the reader every movement in a story. A character may leave a shop and visit a garage. You don't have to take the reader on this walk!

Modernist. This is an adjective which has come to be applied to any type of creative writing which is experimental, mainly with time reference and with the coherence of the plot and character.

Names. Fiction writers take a long time with names of characters. In genre fiction this becomes more important (cf Rhet Butler in *Gone with the Wind*) but normality is the aim in most cases. In satire it might be suitable to give names which suggest qualities, as in Mr. Thwackum in *Tom Jones*.

Opposition: Fiction and poetry both thrive on conflict, adversity and a move towards a harmony in the closure from a disunity at the opening. Thus simple convention is always useful to remember.

Plot: What comes first, plot or character in a short story? Opinions are divided, but try both. Some writers write a profile and a c.v. of their important characters, and say that the people become 'real' in the process of writing. Others plot very carefully and the characters grow from the exigencies of circumstances. Experiment!

Questions:. You might find that the rhetorical question is a powerful stylistic device in articles and journalism. e.g. who knows the answer to the problem of bullying in our schools? The answer is, no one. But the words have a certain force. Interior questions in fiction are effective at times. This is where characters ask themselves questions. (see the monologue work-shop)

Rules: Absolute rules about style were made to be broken, but think long and hard before you do. For instance, the non-sentence - writing a statement given between capital letter and full-stop which has no subject or no finite verb: Wept, again. This is used all the time in fiction. But too much of these creates telegraphese.

Sentences: The basics of a good sentence is that it should suggest a complete action and build on what has happened or what is about to happen. The time-reference and the subject (what you talk about) should be crystal clear.

Tenses: Tenses refer to time. Be consistent. Only change tenses in a story if there is a stylistic reason or effect gained in doing so.

Variety: A simple guideline but always useful - make your statements and verbal effects varied. e.g. Break the basic English word order of Subject- Verb-Object from time to time.

Words. The basic materials of all writing need to be checked and inspected before use. An outmoded word in a story can ruin the whole structure .Absorb the vocabulary of your subject, and also of popular culture and contemporary idiom if you want to write fiction.

Texts referred to in workshops:

1.   Extract from R.L. Stevenson: Random Memories

'Here it was that my first tour of inspection began, early on a bleak easterly morning. There was a crashing run of sea upon the shore, I recollect, and my father and the man of the harbour light must sometimes raise their voices to be audible. Perhaps it is from this circumstance that I always imagine St. Andrews to be an ineffectual seat of learning, and the sound of the east wind and the bursting surf to linger in its drowsy classrooms and confound the utterance of the professor. until teacher and taught are alike drowned in oblivion'.

2.   Written by S. Wade: from 'Villains and Enemies'

'We sat cross-legged in the long hall, filled with excitement because this was that rare thing, a treat: it was something that broke the monotony of dull exercise books, playground fights, censures for 'cheek' and puzzling words from distant, high desks. Imagine the scene: a magic, white screen was produced from a thin red box - a box that resembled a giant pencil. From the pencil rose, like a genie, a white sheet the size of a bus. We were going to see a film and it was to appear, like a genie, from this apparently ordinary tube of red metal. The battle of Bosworth was to burst into the dull hall, the place in which we normally suffered the pains of the circuit training and the leaping over the wooden horse'.

Guide to Writing Performance Poetry
Stephen Wade

Developing Performance Skills-Achieving Success as a Performer

A Straightforward Guide to Writing Performance Poetry is the perfect book for those who wish to develop their poetry and performance skills. The reader is given a firm grounding in the art of performance poetry and the book contains all the basic information needed to develop both writing and performance skills. The material is wide-ranging and adopts a contemporary and novel approach to the art and craft of writing and presenting poetry.

Guide to
Freelance Writing
Stephen Wade

A Comprehensive Introduction to Freelance Writing

This latest book in the Straightforward Guides Series *A Guide to Freelance Writing Revised Edition*, by Stephen Wade, is the perfect book for those who wish to concentrate on writing features, reviews etc. for newspapers and other media. Adopting a methodical step-by-step approach, the book updates and builds on the previous edition. The reader is given a firm grounding in the craft of writing and the book contains all the basic information.

Guide to Writing Romantic Fiction
Kate Walker

Developing Writing Skills-Achieving Success as a Writer of Romantic Fiction

A Straightforward Guide to Writing Romantic Fiction, Revised Edition, by Kate Walker, a leading writer of Romantic fiction, is intended to give the reader a firm grounding in the art of writing romantic fiction. The reader is given an insight into the art of creative writing and the book contains all the basic information needed to develop a successful career.